PLAY LIFE
more

BEAUTIFULLY

PLAY LIFE

more

BEAUTIFULLY

Conversations with Seymour

SEYMOUR BERNSTEIN
& ANDREW HARVEY

HAY HOUSE

Carlsbad, California • New York City • London • Sydney
Johannesburg • Vancouver • Hong Kong • New Delhi

First published and distributed in the United Kingdom by:
Hay House UK Ltd, Astley House, 33 Notting Hill Gate, London W11 3JQ
Tel: +44 (0)20 3675 2450; Fax: +44 (0)20 3675 2451; www.hayhouse.co.uk

Published and distributed in the United States of America by:
Hay House Inc., PO Box 5100, Carlsbad, CA 92018-5100
Tel: (1) 760 431 7695 or (800) 654 5126
Fax: (1) 760 431 6948 or (800) 650 5115; www.hayhouse.com

Published and distributed in Australia by:
Hay House Australia Ltd, 18/36 Ralph St, Alexandria NSW 2015
Tel: (61) 2 9669 4299; Fax: (61) 2 9669 4144; www.hayhouse.com.au

Published and distributed in the Republic of South Africa by:
Hay House SA (Pty) Ltd, PO Box 990, Witkoppen 2068
info@hayhouse.co.za; www.hayhouse.co.za

Published and distributed in India by:
Hay House Publishers India, Muskaan Complex, Plot No.3, B-2,
Vasant Kunj, New Delhi 110 070
Tel: (91) 11 4176 1620; Fax: (91) 11 4176 1630; www.hayhouse.co.in

Distributed in Canada by:
Raincoast Books, 2440 Viking Way, Richmond, B.C. V6V 1N2
Tel: (1) 604 448 7100; Fax: (1) 604 270 7161; www.raincoast.com

Text © Seymour Bernstein and Andrew Harvey, 2016

Cover design: Amy Grigoriou; Interior design: Tricia Breidenthal

Photos of Seymour at the piano on pages ii and 246 by Ramsey Fendall,
courtesy of Risk Love LLC. Photo of Seymour and Ethan Hawke on page 144 by
Eric Zorn. Photo of Seymour's debut with the Chicago Symphony on page 147
by Dr. Baylis Thomas. All other photos courtesy Seymour Bernstein.

Steinway & Sons trademark appears with permission.

The moral rights of the authors have been asserted.

The information given in this book should not be treated as a substitute for
professional medical advice; always consult a medical practitioner. Any use
of information in this book is at the reader's discretion and risk. Neither the
authors nor the publisher can be held responsible for any loss, claim or damage
arising out of the use, or misuse, of the suggestions made, the failure to take
medical advice or for any material on third party websites.

A catalogue record for this book is available from the British Library.

ISBN: 978-1-78180-662-3

Printed and bound in Great Britain by TJ International, Padstow, Cornwall.

Dedicated to Tony Zito
and Ethan Hawke

CONTENTS

WELCOMING WORDS FROM ANDREW HARVEY

You are in for a feast, dear reader. From the first moment I met Seymour—standing in a sleek, dark blue velvet jacket, smiling radiantly in the doorway of Tony Zito's apartment on the Upper West Side—I knew I was in the presence of an extraordinary human being, at once formidable and tenderly approachable. That first unforgettable recognition has only deepened with our friendship. Seymour had come to meet our friend Ethan Hawke for the first time. I shall never forget sitting opposite Ethan and watching him become captivated by Seymour's charm and depth, the two of them leaning so close to each other, they almost touched heads. A year later Seymour played for Ethan, Tony, me, and a small group of friends in his studio. All of us were deeply moved and I asked Ethan to make a documentary on this amazing man, and, to my great joy, he agreed.

If I had to describe the Seymour I have come to know—and that you will come to know in these pages—I would quote something a Taoist friend once said: "A wise man is like jade—hard, indestructible, but softly glowing." I don't know whether I would describe Seymour as hard, but he is certainly, in his essence, indestructible, and I have been deeply moved by the range and subtle rigor of his mind and the profoundly focused clear force of his will. What has come to move me even more about him are the ends to which this inner strength is dedicated—to a sometimes necessarily searing candor, an often hilarious celebration of the quirks of life and human nature, and a constant compassionate outreach to the whole of creation, especially animals. Seymour is forceful and supple, vulnerable and tender. He has an adamantine loyalty to an inner calling and a deep commitment to serving others. I don't know anyone who is more cherished by his friends, and it is one of the great joys of my life that the wonderful documentary by Ethan Hawke has introduced Seymour to hundreds of thousands of people all over the world who now feel intimate with this remarkable man and inspired by his example to live with greater passion and purpose, and to play life more beautifully.

Seymour and I share five great passions—for music, for the healing powers of the spirit, for teaching others in ways that bring out the best in them, for friendship as the most complete and transformative form of love, and a great and abiding love of animals. We are both convivial solitaries, wary of the seductions of fame and success. We are, of course, very different people with different life missions and temperaments, but our souls are linked irrevocably by what we love and revere, and, in each other's presence, the best in both of us flowers exuberantly and with a naturalness that still amazes and humbles us. We both know that, in each other, we have received one of the happiest gifts of our lives, and it is this mutual gratitude that has allowed us, from the magical beginnings of our friendship, to be shamelessly open with each other.

The conversations from which this book was quarried unfolded poignantly, exaltedly, hilariously, over a sun-dazzled week in Seymour's simple wooden house overlooking the sea in Maine. We sat on his sofa in the front room with wildflowers rioting on the ragged lawn outside and the sea constantly shifting in glittering light and spoke for hours, pausing only to go into town for fish and crab cakes and once, unforgettably, to Damariscotta for oysters so fresh they seemed to melt in my mouth. I found myself learning a great deal—about authentic self-love, the mystery of forgiveness, the rigors and responsibilities of all authentic discipline, the miraculous intimacy between animals and human beings, the alchemical creativity of unfettered friendship. I left him after a week feeling both more grounded and elated than I have for years and passionately rededicated to my own work. Sitting on the plane returning home, I realized that I had been speaking with that rarest of beings—a true elder whose teachings and presence are one. Seymour is as much himself feeding an almond to a chipmunk or teaching a Bach toccata, enchanting a thousand people after a screening or sitting in a floppy chair by the sea, hands folded and eyes shut— still a child at 88, awash in wonder.

May all who read this book receive gifts as great, or greater, even, than the ones I have. And may this, our dance together, inspire you to dance even more boldly and joyfully on what a great mystic poet called "God's burning dance floor."

Part I

THE

CONVERSATION

BEGINS

1.

THE FILM:
An Unexpected Blessing

Andrew: Here we are sitting in peaceful bliss in your quiet, rustic house on the edge of the ocean, surrounded by nature, embarking on this exciting conversation together.

Seymour: Of all the things that have happened to me recently, this time with you working on this book together is something I've dearly anticipated.

Andrew: You have just been through a rare and amazing experience. At age eighty-six, leading a relatively quiet life devoted to teaching, composing, writing and playing music, you unexpectedly met the renowned movie star Ethan Hawke, who made a documentary about you, which became a surprising success. Share the story of that life-changing meeting.

Seymour: I never tire of remembering that meeting. Three years ago, my piano pupil Dr. Anthony Zito phoned and invited me to dinner. I'm not the social butterfly type. In fact, I steer clear of large gatherings with people I don't know who sit around sipping cocktails and making small talk. So I asked Tony who else was invited.

He replied, "Andrew Harvey, who lectures around the world and writes about spiritual subjects, and the actor Ethan Hawke. Also, my wife, Diane, and my friend Beatrice will be there."

Frankly speaking, I had heard of neither you, Andrew, nor Ethan, but I was sufficiently intrigued, and accepted the invitation. I then Googled both of you and was astonished at what I discovered: of course I remembered seeing *Dead Poets Society* with Ethan Hawke and being really moved by his acting. But I was transfixed when I saw you sitting at a desk and holding forth on Sacred Activism. You were dynamic.

Andrew: I remember that dinner party vividly, and I especially recall our conversation. I was amazed how freely and easily Ethan opened up to you.

Seymour: The conversation at the table centered on talent, performing, and stage fright. Ethan initiated the subject of stage fright by confessing to the recent crippling effects it had upon him. Having dealt with stage fright myself, and having written a great deal about it in my books, I was able to share with Ethan some valuable information on how to relate to and deal with preperformance anxiety. In the documentary, he actually confessed that I helped him more than anyone else had. During dinner I also put forth an idea very close to my heart. We all know that life influences the way we write, act, or make music. But most people do not realize that the opposite holds true: our talent or artistry, whatever form it takes, defines us and therefore influences our lives.

After dinner both you and Ethan expressed a desire to hear me play. Since I felt more comfortable on my own piano, I invited both of you to my own apartment. But because you were about to travel, and Ethan was involved in a new movie, I had to wait one more year for you to accept my invitation. And actually that was good for me. Having retired from giving public recitals at the age of fifty, I was not in particularly good form pianistically.

Andrew: It's difficult for me to believe that!

Seymour: But it was true! So I practiced diligently to organize an hour-long program for you and Ethan. When I finished playing this intimate recital, you were the first to speak. You arose from the sofa, wiped away some tears, walked up to me, placed your hands on my shoulders, and said fervently in a voice shaking with emotion, "Whether you want to or not, we're making a documentary on you. And Ethan will direct it."

That's how it all started. Little did I know that I would soon be engaged in a project that would change my life in ways that I could never have imagined. Ethan, fascinated by the idea that our talent represents the essence of who we are and can therefore influence our lives, framed the documentary around this theme. He came up with the following title: *Seymour: An Introduction*. The messages within the film are now spreading throughout the world.

Andrew: And now the film has been released, and suddenly you are flying all over the country going to film festivals, receiving standing ovations, being interviewed in the press. And who knows, maybe an Oscar nomination!

Since the opening of the film, your life has taken an over-whelming new turn. What was your life like before we all met at that dinner party in New York, which changed everything?

Seymour: It's interesting that you ask that question, dear Andrew, because I have been thinking a lot about this. Of course being the subject of a documentary that was directed by a world-famous movie star was, at first, like a dream from which I fully expected to awaken. I walked around in a trance for months on end. I used to tell every-body that the documentary changed my life, and indeed it is true, but that's not the whole story. In a way the doc-umentary is a continuation of everything that has gone before. What I mean is, I have always been surrounded by accolades and love, and appreciation for what I do. The press has also been exceedingly kind to me. While the documentary has increased all of this tenfold, it has not changed my life so drastically.

I'll give you an example: When I performed solo recit-als in halls much larger than the auditoriums where the screenings take place, I often got standing ovations. And when I give master classes, the adulation I receive from the teachers and students is similar to the audience responses after screenings of the documentary, except that it's much more intense. But it's in the same category. So, I have a feeling as though the documentary was ordained as a clos-ing element in my life, an extravagant form of praise and recognition in contrast to what I might expect after giv-ing a master class in New Jersey, for example. Just think, Andrew, I'm speaking about global accolades, some of which are overwhelming to me. But as I said before, that aspect isn't so different from what I have already experienced. The real change is that I have become a movie star at eighty-eight!

Andrew: Three weeks before we met in November of 2012, what did you imagine your older age was going to be like?

Seymour: Oh, I would just do more of what I had always been doing, delving into the sacred art of music more and more. I always had the feeling ever since I quit giving solo recitals and got rid of all the tension associated with it that my playing and understating of music has deepened. This gives me enormous pleasure because I can then pass on what I learn to my pupils. A major goal for me has always been a need to make a contribution. I find that when I generate understanding of something in a pupil or a colleague, I have the feeling that I am fulfilling my life's purpose. In turn, it makes me feel good about myself.

People might find it to be an ego trip to say "I love myself," because self-criticism is more normal to most people than self-love. Loving yourself is analogous to recognizing the good and bad aspects of one's playing. I don't think we should toss away our best playing by simply saying, "I'm having a good day." If we don't know why we're playing beautifully, we won't be able to reproduce it where it really counts—in performance. In addition we can easily learn to hate ourselves by only concentrating on the things that don't work, criticizing ourselves and focusing on our failures rather than recognizing the good in ourselves and in our playing.

Andrew: So what you were really feeling was that you wanted to continue to go deeper into music and to share what you were discovering, that was what your life was going to be about.

Seymour: That was one part of it. The other part of it was leaving something tangible behind in the form of compositions and writing. I have a lot of articles and poems, for example, that I never even tried to get published. I write them thinking that somebody will discover them when I'm gone. In addition, I have over two hundred performances of live piano playing on YouTube.

Andrew: When it became clear that there was going to be a film made, how did you approach the making of the film? What happened?

Seymour: Well, first of all when you said to me that a film was to be made, my first thought was, *Now, why in the world would they want to make a documentary on the likes of me? What's so special about me? And why would a major star like Ethan want to direct it?* By his own admission during a Q & A session, I heard at least one reason why he decided to make the documentary. As he said, "I always thought that life influences the way I act. But I learned from Seymour that everything I do in acting can influence my life. That had never occurred to me." So I think that is the main thing he wanted to research during the making of the documentary. I believe he was thinking, *What is it about Seymour? How did he achieve this unity of the musician and the person?*

The fact is, all people can achieve this unity. It requires only that you have a passion about something, and not necessarily about a profession, and to develop that passion or interest to the fullest. During the process, all the elements of integration are being developed, namely, your spiritual, emotional, intellectual, and physical worlds. It is important to be aware of how these elements are developed. For then you can direct them into your personal life.

Andrew: I think that Ethan is an exceptionally brilliant and talented person who, like many brilliant and talented people, is on a quest for their deepest self—on a quest to marry what they do with who they are at increasingly sincere levels.

Seymour: In other words, to define their identity.

Andrew: Yes.

Seymour: So, you know what I say in the documentary about one's identity, namely, that in my opinion, the essence of who we are resides in whatever talent we have. By the way, everything in the documentary is spontaneous. There was no script, and no rehearsals.

Andrew: Really!

Seymour: And I've watched the documentary at least twenty times before appearing at the Q & A sessions. It amazes me that when I talked about certain things, it was off the top of my head, so to speak, completely spontaneous. I could never write certain things as succinctly as I spoke about them in the documentary. Whenever Ethan was asked during the Q & A sessions, "What was it like to work with Seymour in making the movie?" he always said, "Seymour always speaks in whole sentences with semicolons and colons along the way." I never realized that I did that.

I firmly believe that everyone has some talent, or some secret desire to explore something in particular. It could be something like sewing, or gardening, or even cooking. It doesn't matter what it is. But I am convinced that whatever talent we have is a key to who we really are.

Andrew: What was it actually like to make the film with Ethan? How did the film get made?

Seymour: Well, you know, I made a video when I was in my thirties. It was a section from my book *With Your Own Two Hands* entitled *You and the Piano*. It was produced by Quin Mathews, who was an anchorman in Dallas, Texas. A devoted amateur pianist, he had recently purchased a Hamburg Steinway and wanted to make a documentary on me. And so we put that section of my book onto film. Of course that film was nothing like the documentary that Ethan had in mind. When the first shooting with Ethan occurred in my studio, my heart was pounding so fast that I wondered if I would be able to speak. On the appointed hour, the doorbell rang, and the staff arrived, namely, Heather Smith, Greg Loser, and Ramsey, the sound and camera crew. My dear Andrew, there was so much equipment and so many cables that I could hardly walk around my apartment. Around a half hour later, Ethan and his wife, Ryan, arrived. It was a special experience to have Ethan in my own studio. After all, he was such a prominent actor. The first thing Ethan said to me was, "Are you nervous?" I said, "Very." "Well," he answered, "you're not the only one."

So he was nervous, too. You see, we were going to have a shoot in my apartment, the beginning of the movie. Did I know what the shoot was going to be about? Not at all. For two and a half years of shooting, I never knew what the shoots were going to be about until the camera started to roll. I think that spontaneity is part of what is so attractive in this documentary. Similarly, here you are with me recording our conversation spontaneously, and I know something miraculous is going to result from that.

To return to the scene in my apartment, Ethan and I began exchanging thoughts as we did when we first met, whereupon Ryan, interjected with "The both of you stop talking this minute! Seymour, get over there on the sofa and stop talking to my husband. Everything you say is supposed to be in the film!" We all had a good laugh over this.

Things were finally ready and we started shooting. I was at the piano, not knowing why I was sitting at the piano, and Ramsey the cinematographer was in front of my window with the camera pointing at my left hand and into the room, and Ethan was sitting in a chair alongside the piano. By the way, you don't see him in this shoot, you only see me. I suddenly heard his voice saying, "Seymour, play something spiritual." So I started to play a Bach transcription. He said, "What was that that you played?" And I told him. Curiously, none of this appeared in the final editing of the documentary. Ethan preserved only what he thought was necessary to make a convincing film. After all, he couldn't keep everything. But that's what the first shoot was like. At first, I was scared to death. By the third shoot, however, I didn't experience a hint of nervousness.

Andrew: So he had the great gift to relax you completely.

Seymour: I don't think he relaxed me. I think I just gained confidence in what was going on and in my ability to survive. I had already survived performances in major concert halls. When you survive once, it's as though supportive arms carry you into the next challenge. In this case, I didn't fall flat on my face so to speak during the previous shoots. So those supportive arms appeared once again.

Andrew: I think one of the things he did was to set you a very dramatic goal, after all, which was to reappear in public almost four decades after you'd left the stage. That was a wonderfully brilliant demand on his part.

Seymour: Well, when we had a discussion before the first shoot as to why he was making this documentary, these were his very words as I recall: "What I want to show especially to young people is how a devotion to an art form can influence a person's life." I told Ethan that's the thesis of my book *With Your Own Two Hands*. More specifically, the book is about how the serious study and performance of music can make you not only into a better musician, but, more importantly, into a better person. Near the end of that meeting, Ethan must have anticipated that what he was about to ask of me would cause a trauma, because he said in the sweetest voice, "I'm a member of a theater group. We don't know very much about classical music. I know you haven't given a solo recital for thirty-seven years, but would you consider giving a recital for my theater group?" I remember turning pale—

Andrew: Terrifying for you!

Seymour: It was terrifying, Andrew, because in a split second I was thrust back into that period of my life that I had rejected. I sat quietly for a moment—you know how the mind works—it seems like minutes are going by, but in only seconds, the thought flashed through my mind,

Why is Ethan asking me to make this supreme sacrifice and come out of retirement and into the spotlight again as a soloist? I thought that the film would show a lot about my teaching and at that point I remembered that stupid adage, "Those who can, do, and those who can't, teach." And I knew right then that I had to show that I can still really *do*. As this flashed through my mind, I heard myself say to Ethan, "All right, I'll do it." When the meeting was over, I went flying back to my apartment, gathered a whole stack of music—I knew exactly what I was going to play—and I started to practice eight hours a day until the filming of that recital, which took place about four months later, in April. Once again, I practiced as though I was going to make my New York debut.

Andrew: How did you choose the music for the recital?

Seymour: As Ethan told me, his colleagues didn't know very much about music. I wasn't going to play the thirty-minute Schumann Fantasie, for instance. However, the last movement seemed perfect, especially since it was associated with a love story. Schumann wrote it for his beloved, Clara, and sent it to her telling her that she was the note of his life, the "secret eavesdropper." I thought the audience might be charmed by that. The other pieces were rather short, and offered a nice variety of moods—a Bach transcription, a Scarlatti sonata, and a Brahms intermezzo. I also decided to include my own composition entitled *Birds*. At the end of the recital, a very fine pianist who was in the audience came up to me overflowing with compliments and said, "How come you didn't include a 'Hawk' in your set of *Birds*?" You know what I did, don't you?

Andrew: You went to Maine and wrote a beautiful piece for Ethan!

Seymour: I did. I composed a piece called "Hawke," spelled with an *e* at the end. I performed and recorded it. It's on YouTube. Ethan was overwhelmed when he heard it.

Andrew: Let's talk about Ethan now because one of the most wonderful things about the film is the very tender, deep, respectful way in which Ethan treats you. Here is a major world star who could so easily have imposed his own dramas, his own life upon the documentary, but the way in which he gives you the full arc of the film really exemplifies true friendship and true respect.

Seymour: I was very struck by that. After over two years of shooting, the documentary was finally edited. Ethan rented a small screening room to show it to me and some invited guests. "The first time you see yourself in the movie," he told me, "you're going to hate it. So please bring friends along with you who will be objective after viewing it." I invited Michael Kimmelman; Bill Finizio; and Junko Ichikawa, one of my favorite pupils who was in the movie; and Hiroko Onoyama from Sony, my friend for over fifty years. Hiroko's mother arranged concerts for me in Japan when I was on a State Department tour in 1960.

Andrew: And that's how you got to play the *Rhapsody in Blue*.

Seymour: No, Andrew, that performance took place in 1955. That year, I gave the premiere performance of Gershwin's *Rhapsody in Blue* in Tokyo in what was then Hibiya Hall. The conductor was Hidemaro Konoe, brother of the prewar prime minister. Imagine the Japanese public hearing that piece for the first time, and with such a prominent figure conducting.

But let's go back to the documentary. So here we all are. We're in the screening room. The lights dim, and as soon as the film started, I realized the very first scene had been shot in my studio a year earlier. At that time, Ethan had gone into the corner of my room opposite my piano.

"Ethan, what are you doing standing there?" I inquired. He never responded to my question, but immediately asked Ramsey if he was ready to roll. That is what the shoots were like. I never knew from one minute to the next what I was to do.

Then Ethan suddenly said to me, "Today I want you to practice for the recital you're going to give for my theater group, and I want you to talk out loud while you're practicing."

"But Ethan," I said, "I never talk out loud when I'm practicing!"

"Well, don't you talk to yourself?"

"Actually, I do," I confessed.

"Well, do it out loud now."

I practiced a Scarlatti sonata and kept missing the jump of an octave. During the process of fixing it, I spoke out loud about the various means I took to correct the mistake. When I saw this footage at the beginning of the documentary, I was so struck that I called out, "Ethan, that's amazing!" Michael Kimmelman, sitting in front of me, turned around decidedly annoyed and exclaimed, "Shut up, I'm listening to your movie!"

So now the movie ended, and I was in tears. My first comment was, "Ethan, you hardly appear in the documentary!" And he said, "I appear as much as I wanted to."

Andrew: What do you think Ethan's journey has been with you? I've known Ethan for six or seven years. I've been very moved by a quality of deep, passionate hunger to be both an authentic artist and a profound and unified human being.

Seymour: I had the feeling after meeting Ethan at dinner that he was searching for something, and not making progress in what he was searching for. I think he made the documentary not just for me, but also for himself.

Andrew: Very much so.

Seymour: I believe that he sensed in me a quality that he was searching for, namely, the ability to unite the artist and the person. With me, the integration happened automatically through my working at music. For most people, however, it has to be a conscious activity. You have to pay attention to your emotional, intellectual, and physical worlds and how they become synthesized as you work on your art. In my opinion, you can more readily achieve this synthesis in your artistic world because the social world is too unpredictable. It all happens more easily when you are alone with your art, with your practicing.

Andrew: And do you feel that Ethan was intrigued by this marriage of the deep personality with the craft?

Seymour: Yes, Andrew, I believe that he was searching for that integration. In making the documentary, he wanted to discover how it occurs.

Andrew: In a way he was looking for a teacher. And he found in you a teacher that resonated with his soul. His genius was to create a film in which he gives the teacher he found to everyone.

Seymour: Above all I'm a teacher, I've been teaching since I was fifteen. At the time that I met Ethan, I was eighty-six. That's a long time for teaching, right? A pupil who also teaches asked me one day, "How do you know what to tell a pupil after they play for you?" Nobody ever asked me that question before. But I knew instantly the answer: "Oh, that's very simple. You become your pupil. You take on all the aspects of the pupil that you can, his or her emotional, intellectual, and physical worlds. Then, you say to yourself, *How can I improve my playing?* At that point, you will know what to tell them."

I believe that Ethan sensed this. He knew that when he was talking about his stage fright I was filled with the deepest empathy for him because I've experienced stage fright myself. All performers suffer preperformance anxiety to a certain extent. I can't say that it's crippling with everyone, but performers know about stage fright. So what's the big deal? In order to survive, you have to practice in such a way that you perform your best in spite of the stage fright. You can't get rid of it. You accept it as a part of what it is that you have to do. You are about to do something superhuman. As a musician, you are going to perform a complex piece of music from memory in front of a huge audience; as an actor, you not only need to memorize the words of Shakespeare's *Macbeth*, but you have to embody them with your full emotions. The process helps us to transcend ourselves. What a responsibility! Of course it makes you nervous. You think to yourself, *Am I really worthy of doing this? Am I prepared to do this?* If you're humble, it has to make you nervous. Ethan knew we shared this experience due to my discussion of stage fright.

During the dinner, I was very bold and asked him, "What form does your nervousness take?" And he looked at me in great surprise. Do you recall what he said?

Andrew: No.

Seymour: He said, "I have a feeling I'm going to stop talking."

Andrew: Yes.

Seymour: In other words, memory slips. So I was quick to tell him of an article that appeared in *The New York Times* one day. A poll was taken of world-famous performers. What makes you nervous? And it was agreed, unanimously, eighty percent of nervousness is caused by a fear of memory slips.

So, here's Ethan. He has a crippling nervousness that he's going to have a memory slip. He plays parts that require a huge amount of memorizing, just to get the lines down. It's similar to me performing a sixty-page Beethoven sonata from memory—it's an overwhelming responsibility! So I told him the story of Michael Rabin. He was one of our great violinists. Unfortunately, he died in his thirties. Michael Rabin had an accompanist by the name of Mitchell Andrews, who was a friend of mine. At the height of Michael Rabin's career, he suddenly developed a phobia that he was going to drop his bow. And it started to have an adverse effect upon his performing. So one night, he had enough of this. He pointed to a place in the music and said to Mitchell Andrews, his accompanist, "Mitchell, see this chord? Right after you play it, I'm going to drop my bow. So be prepared." So during the performance he played flawlessly until he reached that chord. Then he let go of his bow. Clunk! Onto the stage. The audience froze in terror. There was a moment of silence. He bent down, picked up his bow, and said to himself, *Look at this, I'm still alive.* And he played the piece from the beginning to the end with a roaring ovation. Never had the phobia again. I told this to Ethan.

Some weeks later, during one of our shootings, he said to me, "I was just in a play and in the middle of the play, I had a memory slip and I let out a blood-curdling scream. And then I went on with the play. And every member of the audience thought the scream was part of the play. Nobody knew that I had a memory slip." Then he said, "I think I got rid of my phobia."

Andrew: That's a moving and hilarious story. It reminds me of something John Gielgud once said to me: "Whenever I forget a line, I start staring wildly and muttering to myself and the audience thinks I am doing a 'Gielgud.' When I remember what's coming next, I go on *con brio.*"

Seymour: You know I came to a point after many years of performing when I decided to bring my solo career to an end. The only reason I kept at it so long was to use the stage to get over my fear of not being able to meet musical challenges. I knew that conquering musical challenges would make me stronger to cope with all of life's vicissitudes. I actually hated to be on the stage. I already knew that my art and Seymour were one and the same. The fact that I didn't perform my best meant to me that Seymour the person, as well as the musician, weren't integrated. So I decided I was not going to let it go until I could play in public at major venues the way I had envisioned that an artist should play. And guess what—I actually reached that goal. I ended up playing well in spite of my nervousness. When I heard the results of performances on tape, I felt proud of myself. Having achieved this standard, I felt that I earned the right to call my solo career to a halt.

But it wasn't just because I wanted to escape the nervousness. The press and even the documentary make it sound that way. The chief reason was that I taught half of the day to make a living, and practiced the rest of the day. There was no time to be creative, namely, to compose and to write. So when I reached the age of fifty, I thought, *My life is going by. I want to write books and compose. The only way I can do this is to call my solo career to a halt.* When I announced this after my farewell recital at the Ninety-Second Street Y, my family, friends, and pupils were horrified. I did, however, continue to play chamber music at important venues.

And for all those years after leaving the concert stage I have been very satisfied with my life of teaching, composing, and writing. If anyone had told me at age fifty when I left the concert stage that I would become a "movie star" at age eighty-eight, I would have said that was the most absurd thing I ever heard.

Andrew: Being a movie star at any age has its absurdities, I would imagine. But look at you now, enjoying your celebrity like a dolphin enjoys the sea. You were made for this, my dear Seymour.

2.

THE FILM:
Overnight Success After 88 Years

Andrew: The film has truly made you an "overnight success." Such an experience is rare, and in fact often people are lucky to have any success at all in life. And sadly for some, sudden success can end up being not a blessing but a curse—lottery winners who end up divorcing or spending it all and plunging back into poverty. For you the film's success was unexpected and a complete blessing.

Seymour: Everyone was amazed at the reactions to the film. When we were in Telluride at the film festival where the documentary premiered, Ryan rented a four-story mansion for all of us, Heather, Greg, Ryan, and me. There was a lot of anticipation and anxiety flowing between us because none of us knew what the audience response would be like. At any rate, I sat next to Ethan at the premiere in the old opera house. The movie starts, as you know, with me practicing and talking out loud. When I keep missing a leap of an octave I say, "I keep overshooting the runway here," whereupon the audience burst into laughter. I squeezed Ethan's hand and said, "Ethan, they're getting the documentary." The standing ovation that followed the screening was overwhelming. There's a photograph of Ethan and me on the stage looking out to the standing ovation. Ethan is looking at me with pride and happiness. It's to melt your heart. Have you seen that photograph?

Andrew: I have. When you see him, in that photograph, you feel that what really created the film is that love, that depth of pride and respect.

Seymour: So now it's the next morning, and rave reviews download onto our computers and iPads. We were all sitting in the sumptuous living room in utter disbelief. Ethan said to me, "Seymour, you're innocent about the film world. But I've been in it since I was twelve. I've been to one film festival after another, and I can tell you that when the film is over, half of the audience gets up and leaves before the Q & A session. Did you notice that not one person got up in Telluride? They all sat there. And you heard the ovation. You should also know that during my professional life I never read such reviews as we got this morning." The emails flew into my iPad as friends and pupils read the reviews. We were all knocked out.

I forgot to mention that after the screening, we were all walking on the cobblestoned street towards a restaurant to have lunch. Along the way, two women and a man flung themselves into my arms and wept on my shoulder. Ethan saw this. So we knew that we were facing a hit. That was the beginning of it all. And you know what? It remained like that. Our documentary is the only movie on the website Rotten Tomatoes that has one hundred percent rave reviews.

Andrew: I remember you telephoned me after the film's opening in Telluride and said that after they'd seen it, people fell into your arms in tears of appreciation. You must've understood that something rich and deep was going on in the film.

Seymour: Both Ethan and I were completely stunned. We couldn't believe that people would be so moved. As you know, a year has gone by, with lots of screenings, rave reviews, and accolades. A repeated response from the people who come up to me after the screenings is "I'm not a musician, and I don't know anything about music, but everything you say in the documentary concerns me."

Andrew: What do you think they mean?

Seymour: For one thing, I believe it means that some people don't take seriously enough the activities that interest them, the activities that spring from their individual talents. It doesn't have to be music; it could be anything, anything for which they have a passion. Another is, there are people who had a passion for something, and gave it up. For example, a woman came up to me during the intermission of a concert in New York and said, "I saw your film, and I used to be a writer. I haven't written for ten years. But after seeing your film, I awakened the next morning and started to write again." Something in the film lets people know that it's not too late. Here I am at eighty-eight, and I'm still going strong. I keep saying over and over again in the Q & A sessions what scientists tell us: that, barring brain damage, the older we get, the more capacity we have for learning. In other words, we can therefore achieve even more progress in older age than when we were younger. Now that the documentary has gone global, this message is being projected to more people than I can imagine. It inspires some people to have the courage to pick up the remnants of their passions—if they've abandoned them—rekindle them and make themselves happy again.

Andrew: When you pick up a passion again, it can be a very frightening thing, because you've let it fall. How do you feel your presence in the film reassures people that they can?

Seymour: Well, look what I did in the film: although I hadn't given a solo recital for thirty-seven years, I survived pretty well. Andrew, you know I'm eighty-eight, so you don't want me to lie, do you?

Andrew: No.

Seymour: I think I played gorgeously in that recital. But you don't know what it cost me to play like that. I told you previously that, whether we want to admit it or not, we perform the way we practice. In spite of that, I have known musicians even younger than I am who stopped performing in public for different reasons, and made a comeback with disastrous results. In most cases, when you don't perform in public for so many years, that is what happens. So what measures did I take? I practiced eight hours per day. In order to survive, you have to be twice as prepared as you think you need to be: I had one tryout after another in front of different privately invited audiences; I recorded my recital together with the comments I intended to make; I listened to playbacks, changed interpretive attitudes, re-fingered some passages, and, in short, I did everything possible to survive. So would you like to know how I felt when I came to the hall?

Andrew: Yes!

Seymour: I took a taxi to Steinway with my friend Bill. Did you know that Steinway on West Fifty-Seventh Street no longer exists? They moved to a new location. That probably was the last event in a showroom that reputedly was one of the most beautiful piano showrooms in the whole world. It looked like the interior of a palace. There was a big picture window in front of the showroom facing West Fifty-Seventh Street, so people walking by could look inside and see the events going on. As I got out of the taxi, my heart began pounding. I was a nervous wreck—ready to be taken to the hospital. But, I crossed the street and paused in front of the picture window. The first thing I saw were well-known actors and actresses sitting there, and a host of friends and pupils. I saw Ethan walking around. Finally, I saw the piano bathed in a light so intense that it looked as though the sun had set upon it. Technicians were placing microphones inside the piano and apart from it, and there were cameras everywhere, including one in the balcony way behind the piano. I thought, *There's no way I can survive this.* It would have been difficult enough even if a movie wasn't about to be made. But it would be filmed for posterity. I thought, *This is where I'm going to die. I'll come in and have a heart attack. But at least I'll die in a musical setting.*

Andrew: And on film too!

Seymour: And very dramatic! At any rate, as I entered the rotunda, Ethan gave me a hug, and everyone I knew came over to greet me. Like most performers before major appearances, I pretended that everything was fine. This is what performers really do. You never know that they're nervous, and you certainly don't know that they feel they're going to die. I perched myself on a beautiful armchair as Ethan walked over to me and began speaking: "I want to tell you why I brought you all here," and the event formally began. Andrew, would you believe that as soon as Ethan began speaking, a deathly calm came over me? I thought, *What a relief; what a blessing.* I remember wondering, *Why did this calm come over me?*

Andrew: What was the answer?

Seymour: The answer came the following day: I suddenly realized that I had done this for Ethan in gratitude for all he was doing for me. There was no way I would let him down. I heard myself speak in the documentary before I even played. I said, "You didn't tell them about Sarah Bernhardt and her nervousness," and there's no quiver in my voice. I sounded perfectly calm. I brought that calmness to the piano, and I played the recital straight through without splicing. I never heard of anyone giving a professional concert that's being videotaped or put into a movie without retakes. It just doesn't happen. Performers make mistakes and you have to do some splicing. I did make a few mistakes, but they were insignificant. Days later, I contemplated how I could have experienced something close to a panic attack one minute and then grow deathly calm the next. Here is my conclusion: when you do something for someone else, it temporarily distracts you from your own vulnerability. And that's what happened to me. I performed for Ethan.

Andrew: What I have learned on my journey, Seymour, is that authentic service is selfless, attuned to others completely and not to any private agenda. So you were truly serving Ethan and honoring him and all he had done for you. It reminds me of something a Buddhist sage, Saraha, is said to have written: "This is myself and that is another. Be free of this illusion of separation which imprisons you and your own self is thereby released."

You released yourself by devoting what you did to Ethan.

Seymour: Yes, Andrew, I played every note to Ethan. Now that it's over, I wonder what would have happened had I stopped playing in sheer panic. I wonder if Ethan contemplated this. If so, he must have been more relieved than I was when it was over, and that it had been a success. At the end of the recital, we had a little discussion with the audience about finding one's identity and nervousness. And then it seemed as though the entire audience came over to me at once. Finally it was time to leave. Ethan and I walked arm in arm across Fifty-Seventh Street to the Russian Tea Room. Ramsey, the cinematographer, filmed us from behind. When I saw the documentary, those shots weren't included. The staff was secretly saving those shots. They're going to include the entire recital on DVD after the documentary, and our victory walk to the Russian Tea Room will close the entire presentation.

Andrew: How beautiful! It's lovely to hear you talk about that recital and that moment of calm and how you played the recital for Ethan, because it really deepens my understanding of why people come to you with such joy at the end of the film.

Seymour: It fills me with humility and with enormous gratitude. I believe that when audiences see the documentary, they will respond to my message. In spite of the fact that I'm not a genius, there must be something in my presentation that inspires people. I believe it gives them courage to pursue their gifts, even though they are not geniuses. We can only do the best we can with what we are endowed with.

Andrew: What you're conveying is the absolute importance of owning one's deepest passion and living it. This has nothing to do with whether you're a genius or not; this has everything to do with whether you're going to fulfill the meaning of being on the earth or not.

Seymour: And to do it with whatever gifts you have.

Andrew: Exactly.

Seymour: This is what I tell my pupils: they listen to someone on YouTube and tell me, "Did you hear his tempo? It's so much faster than mine."

"So what if it's faster than you can play," I respond. "You have to choose the tempo at which you can project the proper message of this piece. You need to respect and protect your own talent. You're in competition with no one but yourself."

So pupils have this distorted notion that if they can't play as fast and as accurately as virtuosi, they have no right to play. It's only a question of what you just said: "I want to take my own gifts as far as I can, and that teaches me humility. When I succeed in performing, composing, or writing at a high level of acceptance, it still is a formidable accomplishment for me, even though it can't be compared with the biggest names in the profession. This makes me proud of myself and happy."

Andrew: Even more than that, it's turning up singing your own deep song. And that is the only thing that will make anybody happy.

Seymour: So true.

Andrew: Nothing else makes any of us happy. World fame and huge amounts of money don't make you happy. In my experience, what makes you happy is feeling that your life, at least from time to time, amidst all the shopping, cleaning, and paying of taxes, expresses your deepest truths, your deepest passions.

Seymour: I agree with you completely. I think that this is what they're picking up from the documentary.

Andrew: I think they see someone whom they can truly empathize with because they can see you tormented by stage fright, they can see you in pain about what happened to you in Korea, so they see a human being. But they also see someone who didn't allow his suffering to define his life. And I think that any human being seeing another human being so exposed but so quietly brave is immensely encouraged. We all share the same vulnerabilities and fragilities, but very few of us decide to enact the deepest part of ourselves even though we all know that that's where our true happiness lies.

Seymour: They see me in the documentary acting out triumph over adversity, and they see how much regard I have for my pupils. I love them. It suggests the possibility that audience members can enjoy something like that also. We all have to find the right mentor. Another thing that comes out of the documentary is that we have to take life into our own two hands and not totally depend on anyone else to save us. We have to save ourselves while learning as much as we can from the mentors that we choose to help us.

Andrew: What do you mean "save ourselves"?

Seymour: Well, let's take surviving that performance for Ethan's theater group. Who is going to help me to do that? I have to sit alone in seclusion and work eight hours a day to be sure that I'm prepared to survive the responsibility of doing such a thing. Audiences see this in action, and I think that must inspire them. The message is, "Well, if I can do it, you can do it too."

Andrew: I think the other message is that money is important, and of course you have to put food on your table, but don't forget what your heart is truly inspiring and urging you to do.

Seymour: That's true.

Andrew: Because your way of realizing yourself is very different from the conventional way. You did not choose the grand world; you did not choose money; you did not choose fame. You chose to follow the deepest love in your heart for music, and for helping others.

Seymour: Interestingly, what you just said is confirmed by something in the film, something that I actually resented. But Ethan insisted that I do it anyway. I'm speaking about the scene where I fold up my sofa bed. I think Ethan wanted me to do that to show the audience that I still live in a one-and-a-half-room apartment and that I don't even own a bed, and that my art is more important than material comfort. To say the truth, I continue to live there because it saves money. That allows me to waive my fee for gifted but poor pupils and to pursue my art.

Andrew: And on a deeper level, what that shows is that you have made real sacrifices for what you feel is really important.

Seymour: Absolutely.

Andrew: And I think that a lot of people are very moved by that. They perhaps feel that life has swept them away from their authentic purpose, and when they see somebody who's prepared to make the sacrifices to realize their true self, they feel tremendous admiration and respect and tenderness for that person. But also they feel guilt at what they themselves have not been able to do. The beauty of how you come across in the film is that you don't lay a trip on anybody. You exude the perfume of someone who's found deep serenity from real love. And that invites people, however many times they've given up on their deep selves, to go back to that deep self and renew their acquaintance with it and to choose it.

At Rumi's tomb in Konya there's an inscription which says, "Come, come, whoever you are, however many times you have broken your vows, come, come, come. Ours is the kingdom of joy." I think part of the beauty of your film is that you embrace the all-encompassing love and joy that comes when you really do fulfill your purpose so that people can feel enticed to reenter that deep game themselves.

Seymour: I think that one of the reasons why a lot of people weep when they come to me after seeing a screening is because they're consumed with guilt for not having made the right choices in their lives. But their tears are also of happiness because they see by my example that it's not too late. A man stood up during one of my Q & A sessions and said with a loud, victorious voice, "I saw your documentary and I just want you to know that it changed my life." He then abruptly sat down. I found that deeply stirring. After all, what are the primary reasons for being alive, Andrew? I know you agree with me when I say that our mission is to ease the suffering of people in whatever way we can. People suffer a lot, and something in the documentary suggests ways to ease suffering. The primary thing is to latch on to something that interests you and stick with it until some fruition takes place in whatever your interests are.

Andrew: That's true.

Seymour: Now, Andrew, do you suppose that the documentary would have had the same impact, if I were, say, fifty years old instead of eighty-eight?

Andrew: Of course not. But I'm fascinated about what you think.

Seymour: I do think that my being older is a major factor in how the film affects people.

Andrew: And why do you think being old gave you such freedom and authority in the documentary? Why do you think people are more moved by you old than they would have been in your fifties?

Seymour: Because everybody thinks that old age is a time of decay and the waning of abilities and power, and now they see an eighty-eight-year-old man coming out of retirement after thirty-seven years and giving a recital, going on teaching, and bouncing up the stairs onto the stage and talking coherently. Perhaps they're thinking, *I ought not to be so afraid of growing old. Look what that man does.*

Andrew: I think too that people are famished for the tenderness and compassion and wisdom and tolerance of authentically wise older people. After all our culture celebrates beautiful young bodies, stars of the latest film at the cinema. It celebrates very banal forms of success. In ancient cultures, old people were revered; they still are in tribal cultures.

Seymour: Yes, I know.

Andrew: So in a way Ethan has has smuggled in our ancient longing to be with a real elder, in the form of this documentary, and that's what people are responding to. They are responding of course to all that you teach about how you can age with grace, but they're responding to something even more magical: they're responding to what an old person should be like. Someone who's truly lived a rich life, really loved his life, and grown saturated with serene self-acceptance. That's what an elder is, that's what an elder is destined to show people, and that's what you do. And in our culture, we very rarely have the opportunity to sit with someone like that. So it may be that you're a piano teacher, that you're Seymour Bernstein, that you've had this fascinating life, but there's something beyond that that people are drawn to, and it's this.

Seymour: Yes, of course, I understand that.

Andrew: People are hungry to be accepted and loved for who and what they are by someone who has lived through the whole damn story. And that is what you give them in the film. Everybody knows from the way in which you sit down with your pupils, to the way in which you talk to Ethan, to the way in which you address the camera, that you are somebody with whom they could be and feel deeply seen. And this fulfills one of the deepest longings in the human heart, to meet someone who can truly look at you and see you.

Seymour: Now, Andrew, having said all of that, can you picture how I feel knowing that those messages are being transmitted globally? Imagine how many people will benefit from that? It's overwhelming; it's such a privilege. And you and Ethan made it possible.

Andrew: What I love though is that you began this whole conversation by saying, "In a way it's totally amazing what happened, but in another way it's an extension of what has already happened in my life."

Seymour: It's true. Whereas I've had enormous pleasure from my life before the documentary, with lots of love and accolades, it's expanded beyond my wildest imagination. And with it, my gratitude has expanded by geometric proportion.

Andrew: You may have had accolades before, but to be accepted and loved in this way globally surely is a mirror to you about something very mysterious that has happened to you.

Seymour: I must admit to you that it's not mysterious. As I said earlier, it is an extension of something that has been going on for most of my adult life. As the proportion of the response increases, so does my sense of humility. I have to use the word *humility* because I never think of myself as such an important figure. When I find out that I'm making such a contribution, my gratitude knows no bounds.

Andrew: Because your deepest desire has always been to be someone who contributed, and now through a series of magical transformations, your life, your vision, your understanding of the world is moving hundreds of thousands of people.

Seymour: I know. Isn't it amazing? Well, look at you. You've had more than thirty books published, and you travel around the world and teach. You do for people exactly what this documentary is doing.

Andrew: I hope that something of what you say is true, but I'm still in my early sixties. I think everything that you are giving has the authority of your age behind it. Recently I spent about five days with the Dalai Lama, who just turned eighty.

Seymour: Oh, you met the Dalai Lama?

Andrew: I've met him many times, and I just recently spent five days being taught by him.

Seymour: Oh, did you really?

Andrew: It was amazing! I have known him for thirty-five years. He's always been extraordinary; he's always been this lovely and tender and brilliant being. But now, as he comes towards the end of his life, something even more wonderful has come into him, an even deeper level of wisdom, an even deeper level of love.

Seymour: He's transcended.

Andrew: He's traveling even deeper into the mystery of life. I'm aware that I have an effect on people, but I'm also aware that I'm only three-quarters through my life. There's a huge evolution yet to come.

Seymour: In terms of evolvement, you're still a baby.

Andrew: I'm still a baby and I have a lot to learn, especially from you, especially from the kind of person that life has made you. Everybody feels comfortable with you; there's nobody seeing the film that doesn't feel that they would be loved and accepted by you. I'm not sure that's what I give to people. I think I have intensity and passion, which moves people. I think my work excites them, but I don't believe that everybody who comes to see me feels loved and accepted by me. In fact I know they don't, and I think that this is a lack in me. I have to work harder to abandon my judgmental self, not be so ferocious as I sometimes can be, to really go deeper and deeper into compassion and humility as I've seen you do. I don't know whether you can have that quality in your sixties, I think it's something that only age and suffering and maturity and the wisdom of real older age can give you. I think that's what you have. That's what gives hope. So you give me hope and you give me something to aim for, something to work at constantly in myself.

Seymour: Now, dear Andrew, I have to say something to you. In these conversations, it seems to me that I'm learning more from you than you are from me. It's the way and the content of how you express your thoughts and feelings. The intensity of it, your choice of words, and your whole presentation in our conversations has moved me deeply. It seems to me that you give me more than what I have given to you. What do you think about that?

Andrew: But wouldn't that be what love would always feel? When you love someone else as we love each other, purely, simply, completely, you always feel that the other is far more beautiful, far more intelligent, giving you far more than you give back.

Seymour: Really? That's how you think love operates?

Andrew: Yes, I do. And I feel that I'm learning so much more from you because I see more and more of you as I get to know and love you more and more.

Seymour: See more of Seymour?

Andrew: I get to see more of Seymour!

Seymour: But after all when two people love each other it could be on the same level, it could be reciprocal.

Andrew: It is reciprocal . . .

Seymour: But my awareness is that you are far more evolved than I am.

Andrew: No, no, Seymour. I have the complete opposite vision. I feel you are much more evolved than I am. But ultimately as long as we can keep this experience of learning from each other going, our conversations need never end!

Seymour: I certainly will do my best in keeping our conversation going.

Andrew: And so will I. Now let's get back to people's reactions to the film, because I think there are two more wonderful themes to explore. Perhaps the first, the most important one is that people feel that you are speaking your complete truth. And they're so unused to that. So you're using the privileges of being older to just say it as you feel it and know it. And this is immensely exhilarating for people.

Seymour: Yes, I'm aware that with my age came a freedom and a conviction to say things as I think and feel them. It's usually against what others expect me to say. I'm convinced that when you speak the truth of your feelings, it's the greatest compliment to another person. I would even call it an act of love to speak the truth of your feelings.

Andrew: Don't you find people respond to that in the film?

Seymour: Yes I do. It's the same in everyday life.

Andrew: I think the other great attractor in the film is what I could only call the spiritual radiance around you. The way in which you present yourself is outside all religion, outside all desire to proselytize; you're simply being your complete self, which involves reclaiming your deep spiritual self, and radiating that.

Seymour: And this amazes me, you know why? Because many of the audience members are followers of a religion. Now listen, I don't spell *god* with a capital *G* because when I contemplate a universe that not only doesn't have an end, but is still expanding, and when I think of life in so many forms, I find it too awe inspiring to believe that an anthropomorphic figure sitting on a throne in a so-called heaven is responsible for all of this. It is beyond my comprehension. I find it insulting to whatever is responsible for all of this. It can't be given a name. It's not given to us to know its name. My concept is a manifestation that is within all living things. I like to call it a *spiritual reservoir.* I think of a *reservoir* being filled with a capacity to answer everything that we need to know and to do in life. We have to consult that *spiritual reservoir* inside of us, and not always depend on a divinity to answer our questions and to help us in need.

Andrew: So you're really asking people to become adults, to grow up, to acknowledge that this enormous reservoir of spiritual intelligence lives in them as a gift, and to claim it, and to work with it consciously—

Seymour: Exactly. As the adage goes, "God helps those who help themselves." Well first of all I never call it "god" because I think it's demeaning to give it a name.

Some years back, I had a pupil who had a revelation and became a Christian. One day at a lesson, he suddenly stopped playing and said to me, "Seymour, I'm really worried about you."

"What are you worried about?" I asked.

His reply astonished me: "What's going to happen to your soul when you die?"

I replied, "Stop worrying about my soul and worry about that Debussy piece that you're playing. I'll take care of my soul."

My pupil actually imagined that if you believe in this figure sitting on a throne, you will go to heaven when you die. And if you don't, it's down to hell with you. I find this concept downright absurd.

In reading from your wonderful books, I discovered that the Buddhists believe neither in god, nor heaven, nor hell. They think that the concept of god originated out of the fear of coming to an end, and that religion had to be created to replace the abyss with hope. Jews also don't believe in heaven or hell.

Andrew: So you don't believe in an afterlife, you don't believe that this consciousness that is Seymour is going to continue?

Seymour: It beats me, baby. I would love to think that I will go on. But I have no idea, and my humility tells me that it's not given to me to know the answer. It's beyond my cognition. I will never know whatever, or whoever, is responsible for the mystery of everything that I perceive, a universe that is still expanding, and multiple life-forms. I believe there cannot be answers to these questions.

Andrew: And you don't seem to need an answer.

Seymour: No, I don't. It's good enough for me just to be in awe of it, to be on my knees in wonderment. See that tree outside? It's another life-form. And when nobody is looking, I wrap my arms around the trunk and I actually have a feeling that our pulses are meeting. I become the tree and the tree becomes me. We're one and the same. While sitting with you, who are such a miraculous spiritual being, gazing at the glorious scenes outside gives me the feeling that we're all united; you and I, the trees, the chipmunks, and the sea are all one. I have a feeling of oneness. And that's good enough for me. I don't have to go further and wonder what's going to happen to me when I die. I actually look forward to death as another adventure. The moment of death must be a profound one. There's nothing to fear. In his poem "Thanatopsis," William Cullen Bryant wrote about death in a beautiful and comforting way:

So live, that when thy summons comes to join
The innumerable caravan, which moves
To that mysterious realm, where each shall take
His chamber in the silent halls of death,
Thou go not, like the quarry-slave at night,
Scourged to his dungeon, but, sustained and soothed
By an unfaltering trust, approach thy grave,
Like one who wraps the drapery of his couch
About him, and lies down to pleasant dreams.

In my estimation, poetry is close to music in its ability to capture the essence of human thoughts and feelings. I have composed a lot of poems. Do you write poems too?

Andrew: Yes, yes.

Seymour: Life gets encapsulated in a poem in the most intense way. And when you get to the end of the poem, with the last word, the profound meaning of the poem seems to explode upon our consciousness. Every word along the way is building up towards this profound meaning.

Andrew: Do you have a favorite poet? Do you have someone you love the most?

Seymour: Well, everybody loves Rilke, right?

Andrew: Yes.

Seymour: But I've read other poems in your books. You have poems from different centuries and poets that I've never heard of. And look at Sappho in ancient Greek times. My late friend Flora Levin was a classicist and she translated ancient Greek manuscripts. Did you know she taught me how to write? Let me tell you a wonderful story about her. It was with her help that my book, *With Your Own Two Hands*, was written. Finally it was completed and about to be published by Macmillan. I hope I don't cry in the middle of what I am about to tell you, because the story is still overpowering to me.

I was teaching one day and Flora phoned me. "You know," she said, "I never interrupt your teaching, but I know your book is at the printer and you've got to stop your teaching and call the publisher to stop the press."

"Flora," I responded, "what are you talking about?"

She said, "I don't have the time to tell you, it will be too late. Just do what I tell you and I'll explain later. Just do it!"

I hung up; I called my editor, and asked him to stop the press. They were about to print five thousand copies of my book, and they did suspend the printing. I called Flora back and asked her why she had me do this.

"Now I will tell you. I was translating ancient Greek manuscripts, and I came upon the following poem by Sappho that had never been translated into English:

> I never dreamt
> that with my own two hands
> I could touch the sky."

I simply burst into tears. Flora had found a poem by the greatest woman poet in antiquity that had almost word for word the title of my book, *With Your Own Two Hands*. So I called the publisher and they inserted it on the first page of the book. They were so moved by it. They couldn't get over it. If Flora hadn't phoned when she did, the book would've been printed without that poem.

Andrew: Amazing, amazing.

Seymour: Only three lines, and imagine the impact of that poem. I remember reciting the poem into the cameras. I wondered what Ethan was going to do with it. It speaks volumes for his sensitivity that he placed it at the end of the documentary. Many people burst into tears at that point. One reviewer stated, "You can't remain dry-eyed at the end of the movie." Even I started to cry because of the import of that poem.

Andrew: Perhaps that's the most profound reason of all that people are so drawn to you in the film. They see in you somebody who has touched the sky. And what you're saying and showing us is that you can do this in the middle of your ordinary life if you choose the deepest gift and passion that lives in you. That's a hugely hopeful message for people. It gives them a sense that whatever's happened in life, the pain and the difficulty and the bewilderment, and perhaps the lack of so-called "success"—in spite of all this, the real truth of life, this touching the sky with your hands, is always accessible to them.

Seymour: That is why Ethan wanted to make the documentary. He wanted people to know that a deep involvement in something they are passionate about can influence their lives and help them to touch the sky.

PART II

MUSIC

1.

THE MAGIC OF MUSIC

Andrew: Seymour, talking about the film and the excitement and deep meaning of the whole experience has been wonderful. But let us now turn to your lifelong passion. What is music for you?

Seymour: Nobody knows what music is. The greatest thinkers in the world have tried to define the miracle of music. Why, for example, does it make us feel the way we do? You know what Plato said: "Music penetrates the inner-most regions of the soul." Imagine when that was said, in ancient Greek times. So we know that music has always moved people deeply. There's something about organized sound that can trigger every emotional response experienced by humans. And there are some responses that we can't describe in words. But we feel them and know that they exist. The other thing is that we're aware of an order and a harmony within music's structure that permeates us and makes us want to be like it. When I'm playing any piece of the great masters, I have a feeling that I would like to be as organized, structured, and communicative as the music is. Music, for me, is an example of what I should be like. And I try to transmit that concept to my pupils. If only we could be like music is, it would benefit us tremendously. So what is music? Perhaps a simple answer might be that music is a language of feeling. Whatever music is sincerely written, highly organized, and communicates something deep and personal, I would want to be like it is. And this is not just for classical music. For example, one of my favorite pieces is "Hallelujah" sung by Jeff Buckley.

Andrew: Each of the great composers has a different sound and emotional world. So how do you experience your favorite composers when you're playing them, how do you experience their ideal world? Could you put that into words for me?

Seymour: Well, it's very true what you say. Each composer expressed their feelings in a particular language. It would be like a German, a French, and an Italian writer would write about ecstasy. They would use different words to describe how they feel about ecstasy, but in order to know the meaning, we would have to know their language. The miracle of music is that even though Bach and Rachmaninoff were born in different centuries, and lived in different parts of the world, nevertheless, their music communicates the deepest feelings. That's the miracle of music. It's ageless. It doesn't matter that it's from a different century. The message comes out clearly. Schumann inserted a motto at the beginning of his Fantasie referring to a "secret eavesdropper." Well, musicians are secret eavesdroppers. We get the message. Not everybody will, but musicians do. Music is really a universal language.

The amazing thing is that natives in Borneo have the same feelings that we have. In 1960, I went on one of many State Department tours and was the first pianist to give recitals in Borneo. A wealthy Chinese lumberman did business with the headhunters. It was only ten years since they had refrained from lopping off heads. He took me ten miles down a tropical river to visit the headhunters in their long houses. I saw shrunken heads strapped to poles, which sent shivers down my spine. The chief took us into his room and gave us a drink of some awful-tasting stuff. While we were chatting, I saw to my amazement a portable phono that you wind up, and old seventy-eight rpm records strewn around a table. They were recordings of Beethoven, Schumann, and other greats. Can you believe this so-called primitive loved classical music? It's because of what I said before: the miracle of music is that its language is universal.

Andrew: So let's look at the great composers that I know you love and let's look at you as an eavesdropper on their message. When you eavesdrop on Bach, what do you hear? What is the message of the greatest of all composers to us?

Seymour: I would say, in general, that most of their messages make me want to weep. There is a preponderance of sadness in the music of master composers. I'm not alone in this thought. Many sensitive musicians agree with this. I'm not speaking about people who just listen to music, but rather people who perform music on an instrument or through singing. Performing is quite different from listening, because there is a body language involved in the process of absorbing music's meaning. Of course the great composers project joy as well, and, in short, all human emotions. The great composers have also captured the beauty in nature in their compositions. My late friend Flora Levin thought that musicians are philosophers since they search for the truth of things. And so the great composers found a way to organize sound so as to capture the essence of human feelings.

Andrew: Bach has tremendous joy in his music, great exaltation, and celebration of the cosmic dance. So music has this tremendous capacity to initiate us into the grief of life, what Virgil called "the tears of things." But it also has a similarly vast gift to initiate us into the ecstasy of life, the cosmic joy of the dance. It's both, isn't it? In fact, of course music has the power to evoke every kind of state and feeling, anger, tenderness, bewilderment, aching nostalgia . . .

Seymour: It encapsulates every emotion known to humans. But the reason why I said sadness first is because it seems to me that that's the predominant feeling.

Andrew: Schubert said, didn't he, that all great music is sad.

Seymour: Did he say that?

Andrew: Yes.

Seymour: And of course Schubert's music also encapsulates joyful singing, not only through pitches, but also through rhythm.

Andrew: For me, music is a mirror in sound of a mysterious, organizing Intelligence in the universe. Music is the disembodied but miraculously potent representation of an Order that is bubbling in everything and expressing itself as the unfolding of everything.

Seymour: I'm not completely convinced of that. Let's start with composers: Bach and Beethoven have been called godlike. But they were not gods; they were humans, just as we are. They were imbued, however, with gifts that transcend anything that we could imagine. Talent of that caliber is inborn. Scientists have even pinpointed the *planum temporale* as the place in the brain where talent resides. They claim that that portion of the brain is enlarged at birth in someone with exceptional talent. The truth is you can't teach someone to become a Mozart. One has to be born a Mozart. Naturally such gifts have to be drawn out of such geniuses through education. If one agrees that these so-called godlike figures were mere humans, then it follows that the music they created represents an emanation of human feelings. The composers may have been influenced by the concept of the universe and everything associated with nature, but they specifically express human feelings that we all recognize and experience. And that's what moves us so about their music. We don't have to think about it. It simply triggers our emotional world. By the way, scientists do know that music is processed in a part of the brain over which we have no control.

Andrew: Really?

Seymour: It activates us without thought. Not like a philosophical concept that has to be thought out. Experiments have been performed to prove this. For example, scientists have gone into wards in asylums where schizophrenic patients can't be reached through language, and where they are very lazy about making up their beds in the morning. March music is piped into the ward, and the patients' feet start automatically tapping rhythm—one, two, three, four. It's because adrenaline courses through their bodies. The result is that they make up their beds in half the time.

Andrew: And of course music has been used for healing in many societies. Islamic cultures employed music as a way of healing psychiatric disorders; there were lunatic asylums in the sixteenth century in Europe that used music as a way of calming patients and easing them back into their right minds. What do you feel about music therapy?

Seymour: Music therapy became a profession around the time that I was in my twenties. And would you believe, Andrew, that I was involved in music therapy before it became a profession? I was invited to give a recital in an institution in New Jersey. I was on a stage, and all of the patients sat in a formal auditorium with attendants all around them. I was told that at the end of the recital, the psychiatrists wanted to talk with me about how music affected me during my practicing and what I thought of music as a possible aid in getting through to their patients. At that time, little was known about the effects of music on disturbed people.

The last piece on my program was Chopin's Polonaise in A-flat. While I performed it, a woman flew out of her chair and headed for the stage. She was beating a rolled-up newspaper in her hand and screaming, "Play on, play on!" Every attendant in the place closed in on her. I heard her scream, and then silence. They took her away. Clearly, music aroused deep emotions in this patient. I discovered that her name was Adelaide, and that she had been a piano major at Juilliard.

After the recital, the doctors put me in the center of a room and they sat around in a circle. They asked me every conceivable question about music. Finally they asked if I would participate in some experiments with patients who used to be pianists. I said, "Of course I would." I kept a diary of this. You can't believe what was accomplished. For example, there was a young man in his thirties by the name of Lloyd. He was a child prodigy. For fifteen years, he hadn't spoken a word. He was an advanced schizophrenic. When they got him to a piano, they would put music in front of him and he would never turn the page. He would just keep playing the same page over and over again, and suddenly look away and play it from memory. He must have had a photographic memory. They couldn't get him to go on. They thought it was symbolic of his not wanting to face the tomorrow of life. They brought him to me, and his psychiatrist sat next to me while I worked with him. I was merely experimenting. He played the first line of something for me, and I took a piece of paper and covered up that line. Then he played the next line. I covered that up, too. He got to the end of the page and I covered up the entire page. His hand went up, and he turned the page for the first time in fifteen years and continued to play. In the next moment, he called me "Seymour." He hadn't been able to speak for fifteen years. The doctor was in utter disbelief.

The thing about mental patients is that they show abnormal rhythm. Lloyd would play a waltz, for example, with a highly distorted pulse resulting in one measure having two beats and another having four beats. I turned on a metronome, stood behind him and pushed him forward on one, and back on two and three. He not only began to play even three beats to a measure, but he also started a conversation with me.

Andrew: How amazing.

Seymour: Music has a tremendous effect upon behavior. As the scientists tell us, it enters the amygdala, a part of the brain where we don't have to think. The amygdala triggers an emotional response. We don't have to think what we're feeling. We know that we're feeling something.

Andrew: As I have grown, and looked at life, I have come to understand that my own life and the lives and destinies of my friends and the life and destiny of the world, what I would call the cosmic unfolding of things, is very much like a fugue. A fugue has a simple theme, and then amazingly intricate variations on that theme. But if you're listening carefully, you can hear the simplicity of the theme being used in all of these wild variations. This corresponds to the way in which nature works, in which temperaments unfold in life. So it seems to me that musical form is more than human discovery. It's mirroring something in reality, and helping us to unite with reality, to experience reality, at a deeper level.

Seymour: Well, I believe that what you're talking about is that everything is united. That's the ancient Greek concept of *one*. Everything is united and we're part of it. I think in simple language, this is what you're talking about.

Andrew: Yes. We were talking about fugues the other day, and you had some wonderful things to say about how a fugue works. For me the fugue is the most revelatory of all musical forms and the one that most expresses the way in which our lives and reality unfold.

Seymour: No one wrote more wondrous fugues than Bach. Musicologists have pondered how he organized them. It is thought that when Bach wrote down a motif for a fugue, he knew from the motif itself exactly what that fugue would be like, how many voices it would tolerate, whether it could bear another subject, and what the countersubject would be. "Subject" and "countersubject" refer to musical phrases (melodies) that interweave throughout the fugue. To this day, I can't get over the C-sharp minor fugue in Book One of *The Well-Tempered Clavier*. It has three subjects (three melody lines). Each one is introduced separately. And would you believe, after they're introduced, all three subjects appear at the same time throughout the rest of the fugue. Vertically, each entry makes perfect harmony. When we compose music, each line of melody flows horizontally. If there are multiple melodies, then harmonies are created where the melody lines cross vertically. So at every point the melodies meet vertically, the harmonies have to make sense. It's an intricate and complex endeavor to make this work. And in the C-sharp minor fugue, all three melodies meet in ecstatic harmony as well as being beautiful melodies in themselves. It symbolizes to me one of the greatest achievements of the human mind.

Andrew: It's almost as if Bach is transcribing the mathematical ecstasy of the creation of all things.

Seymour: But that's exactly what he's doing. Exactly. You said it perfectly.

Andrew: Let's go back to you. I would love it if you would describe your journey into music. How did your passion for music awaken, what was the piece of music that made you suddenly respond?

Seymour: I remember distinctly what it was. I was three years old and my parents took me to visit my aunt Ethel. She was my father's sister. While the adults were talking, I pranced around the room and discovered a large black box. It was, of course, Aunt Ethel's upright piano. I noticed white and black objects on it. I couldn't resist, so I touched one of them. "Bing!" I heard a sound and thought, *What a miracle this is. What is it?* And with my little dimpled fingers, I depressed a series of white and black keys. Tunes floated out of the box. Right then and there, I knew that this was my destiny.

Andrew: You knew at that moment.

Seymour: I knew. I was only three, but I remember distinctly. Between three and six, I began to make up tunes on Aunt Ethel's piano, and I began to listen seriously to all the music I heard around me, especially the music that a teacher played in school when we marched into the auditorium. It wasn't until I was six that someone gave us a player piano. I felt as though my life began at that moment. Do you know how my mother found me a piano teacher? Mr. Robee, our milkman, came in one day to deliver milk and cream for our household.

"Do you know of any piano teacher?" my mother asked him. "My son would like to take piano lessons."

"My daughter teaches," the milkman replied.

That's how my mother found my first piano teacher. Her name was Rita Robee. She charged fifty cents a lesson. She played pieces for me, and I was in awe. I never heard anything so thrilling. She taught me the names of the lines and spaces and left me some beginner's books to peruse. I recall that soon after she left that first day, I discovered that I could sight-read notes instantly.

Andrew: Wow.

Seymour: I don't understand it. I don't remember any laborious process of learning to play the piano. It all made such sense to me: this is here and that's there on the keyboard. And so, I just devoured the books that she gave me at each lesson and played everything from memory without knowing what memory was. My lessons were on Saturday. Around the fifth lesson, she gave me a book of arrangements of famous melodies. The following day, on Sunday, I couldn't wait to read through my new book. So I awakened very early and crept downstairs to the piano. I opened my new book, randomly, and discovered a piece called "Serenade" by someone called Schubert. Andrew, that piece was *familiar* to me. It was like something inside of me that was awakened, something that I knew intimately. I was so moved that I began to cry. It touched me so deeply. My parents and three sisters were asleep on the second floor. My mother was suddenly awakened by the sound of the piano. She came rushing downstairs and found me crying.

"Why are you crying?" she asked.

"Oh Mama, that's the most beautiful piece I ever heard. I know that piece."

Now how do you account for that? I know what you're about to say, "Well, you see that's the indication of a former life."

Andrew: Well, yes, I do believe in reincarnation. I believe we evolve skills and capacities over many lives, and I believe you've had many lives as a musician. In this life you are bringing it all to consummation and giving the essence of what you've learned on your whole journey to people in the way that has flowered in this film, and is flowering in this book.

Seymour: Well, you know Jung thought that we inherit all of civilization, including animals. I guess that's another form of reincarnation, genetic reincarnation. Whatever the explanation is, I found that experience miraculous. My musical adventures continued from that point on.

Andrew: I would love to ask you to unveil the discoveries you made of the great composers. Can you remember the first moment you experienced Schumann, Mozart, Bach? How did your tastes in music evolve? Who was very important for you as a composer when you were young?

Seymour: I have to tell you the truth. Every composer that I was exposed to moved me deeply and became my best friend. I suppose you can say that I was promiscuous, because I loved them all. I couldn't differentiate between them and say, "Oh, I love this one more," because each one was a novelty and a discovery. It's not unlike meeting different people. You love one person and then you meet someone else that you also love. I can't say that I love Bach more than I love Schubert. And I can't say that I love Schubert more than I love Schumann. I love all of them for their own qualities and for their own messages that they have left to the world. I love some Stravinsky. But in general, I have an aversion to atonal music.

Andrew: Then help me by trying to put words to the qualities and the message of these different ones you love. Introduce me to your friends. What is the quality you love in Mr. Bach, Mr. Schubert, Mr. Schumann?

Seymour: All the music that I love has beautiful themes. My love begins with that. I'll never forget when I was introduced to the Bach two-part inventions and I heard the opening motif. And then I realized what he's doing; he's making a whole piece based on that series of notes that constitute the first motif. I couldn't believe it. It moved me so much and amazed me how that motif threads through the entire piece, and every time it comes it has a different feeling about it. So I can't separate the emotional experience from the structural experience. Emotion and craft are synthesized.

I experienced the feelings of certain structural components in music long before I learned what they were called. For example, let's take cadences, or endings: certain ones literally made my mouth drop open in awe. I instinctively delayed the final chord of such a cadence and always played the final chord softer. When I was seven I learned that such a cadence was called a *deceptive cadence* because instead of ending on a one chord, namely, a chord built on the first tone of a scale, it ended on a chord built on the sixth tone of the scale, which gives the impression that the piece is not quite finished because the ear wants to hear a one chord. Now if someone had tried to explain what a deceptive cadence was before I had experienced it, I wouldn't have understood it at all. I deplore education that teaches us analysis before the student experiences the feelings inherent within a structure.

Andrew: What would be your dream plan for musical education in schools? How would you structure musical education?

Seymour: First, everyone has to sing. And everybody has to move their bodies in a dance form according to rhythm. Rhythm and melody are integrated like that. And now you go to the piano and you make up sound dramas such as I did when I was a little boy. A storm is coming:

a rumbling in the bass and lightning strikes—shrieking sounds in the treble—with glissandos and all kinds of configurations. And now the sun comes out and everything is calm and soft. I would always create these sound dramas on the piano. It's called improvisation.

So here is Beethoven, his father is drunk and he's supervising little Ludwig on how to play the piano and read notes. And Ludwig is about ten, and he suspends his practicing and starts to improvise sound dramas, like I did, and a voice comes from the other part of the apartment: "Ludwig, stop that fooling around and get back to your practicing. You can do that fooling around much later in life. First learn how to read notes."

Andrew: So while inviting people to improvise, it's inviting people to discover the roots of music, and to discover there is in all of us a protocomposer.

Seymour: There you are. Organization is after the fact. First, do things spontaneously.

Andrew: How would you introduce someone to the magic of music?

Seymour: Here's a story. I was in California and there was a wonderful girl in my master class who had won every contest in California. She was about to play the Beethoven Sonata Op. 109. I asked her, "What do you think you have to do in order to understand Op. 109?"

"Oh," she said, "The first thing I have to do is find out everything I can about what was going on during Beethoven's lifetime when he was writing that piece."

I said, "What sort of things?"

"Oh, I want to know everything sociological, and also political. All of this I think affected how Beethoven composed Op. 109." I said to her, "Trust me when I tell you that all of that knowledge that you would gain by researching in all of these areas won't teach you how to play the first two notes of Op. 109." She said, "Really?"

I said, "Absolutely really. Those facts are only interesting after you know the piece and have studied it on its musical foundation, and no other foundation."

I suggested that she place her intellectual world in neutral and begin Op. 109 without any preconceived notions. I then asked her to eavesdrop, so to speak, on her various responses. Eventually the music told her exactly what it wanted to do.

I then told her a story about the composer Alexander Tcherepnin. I played his trio once, and so he adopted me. He just never got over the fact that I played his trio. He was the head of the theory department in a major university. On this occasion, a CD came out of his compositions, and I hosted an evening for him and his wife and invited all of my pupils to hear it. It was a wonderful occasion in my apartment. At one point in the evening, Tcherepnin went to the piano and everyone stopped talking. He was evidently going to demonstrate something to a pupil who asked him a question. He played a series of eight very basic chords in a particular sequence. He then turned to us and exclaimed, "I have just reduced Mozart's *Jupiter* Symphony to eight chords. Knowing every one of those chords won't bring you that much closer to the *Jupiter* Symphony." You see analysis is after the fact. It won't lead you to the heart of music.

Andrew: Yes, because if you analyze the music too soon, you prevent people from having the full experience of the music.

Seymour: There it is.

Andrew: That is one of the dangers of modern musical education, isn't it?

Seymour: That's the chief danger.

Andrew: It's so beautiful what you're saying because I remember how I first awoke to the passion of music. It wasn't through analysis or through music being talked about; it was through my grandmother who was a concert pianist, playing in the early morning when I stayed with her. I'd wake up in the early morning to hear her playing Chopin and Brahms, and then I'd sit by her and watch her play with her full, wild, passionate being pouring itself out on the piano. And that was a transmission beyond words of the power of music, which changed my whole life. In fact it made me want to be a concert pianist. I studied the piano under several teachers from the ages of seven to fourteen, when I realized that I was not destined to be the next Horowitz. By then, though, I had discovered the wonder of poetry and novels, so I switched to wanting to be Shakespeare or Dickens, pouring the passion music had awoken in me into writing thousands of bad sonnets and, at fourteen, a truly dreadful novel about a crazy composer who commits suicide during the premier of his first five-hour-long symphony. From my early teens onward, I also studied in increasing depth the various forms of music composition, just in case I was destined to be Mozart, not Horowitz. It was the sonata form that most enraptured me then. I read and reread everything I could find about it, but without that initial, huge transmission from my grandmother, none of that would have meant anything.

Seymour: So when you learned about sonata form, did that add to your enjoyment of music?

Andrew: Yes it did because it made me appreciate that music was so deep an art that it could be at once very ordered and very abandoned, and that gave me an understanding of just how profound the enterprise of composing was. So I think that the first thing that's essential in musical education is to create the conditions for people to have a rich experience of the power of music so that they are strongly motivated to truly want to understand how it comes to be so powerful. Then they can be slowly introduced to the more intellectual analytic elements, but always in the service of opening up the depth of the expressiveness of music.

Seymour: I had two striking experiences along these lines. One concerned a school for prodigies in New York City. A Russian pianist was the director of the school, and there were other Russian teachers on the faculty. A pupil of mine knew a parent whose son went to that school. One day the parent brought her son to play for my pupil, and my pupil found the boy's playing barren in interpretation. He worked with the boy and got him to play expressively. At his next lesson with his Russian teacher, the mother told the teacher about what my pupil did for her son. "Well, you see," the teacher explained, "this is what our method is: we first see to it that our pupils play accurately note-wise, with the proper fingering, and technique, and then we put the interpretation on after that." I was horrified when I heard this.

Andrew: I think it's awful. What was the second story?

Seymour: I cannot mention names because I'm very close to this person. But this person is absolutely one of the real geniuses alive today. He was teaching in a very important school in upstate New York, and I had two pupils going to that school. One day he gave a lecture on the following subject: "How to Arrive at Musical Interpretation Through Harmonic Analysis." In the middle of the lecture, he announced the following: "If your technique isn't finished by the age of twelve, don't even think of having a career as a pianist."

So my two pupils, who were enrolled in that school and aspired to have careers in music, came for their lesson afterwards, and both of them said to me, "Well, what's the point of continuing to practice? My technique wasn't finished at twelve. So I can't hope to have a career." My pupils believed what this man said because he was a famous authority figure. I had to do a major rehabilitation job on those pupils to restore their confidence.

Andrew: What you want to restore to the experience and practice of music is the primacy of the heart's experience.

Seymour: Of course, of course.

Andrew: And that's why people respond so profoundly to your playing and to your presence. But you must be aware that this is, in many ways, an old-fashioned approach to music. It comes from the depths of the tradition; it doesn't sit with the modern, sterile, dissociated intellectual approach.

Seymour: What makes you think it stems from the past? The past was far worse than the present.

Andrew: Really?

Seymour: Terrible, yes, and faulty in the approach to technique. Do you know what they did to prodigies' hands in order to make their fingers independent? They actually severed the skin between the fingers to free them. In many instances, they ruined the hands of children.

You know what Schumann did to his hand? He tried to strengthen his fourth finger, which is trapped by ligaments of the third and fifth fingers growing over the fourth finger. Anatomically, the fourth finger is imprisoned for life. You can never free it. You have to learn how to use rotation to give it power. So Schumann, not knowing these anatomical facts, attached a string to his fourth finger. The string went over a pulley and connected to a heavy weight attached to the other end of the string. Schumann then forced his finger down against the weight at the other end of the pulley and crippled his hand. So he never developed into the fine pianist that he wanted to be.

So you see, in earlier days, it was much worse than today. They started with analysis and with finger approach devoid of wrist and arm movements. It was quite brutal. I don't know how many of the gifted people survived. But Chopin was one of the first to free everyone. Judging from the various accounts of his playing and testimonials to him from his pupils, I conclude that he was one of the first pianists to use forearm rotation and undulating wrists.

Andrew: What I meant was, at the beginning of the twentieth century, if you listen to how pianists play Chopin, Brahms, or Beethoven, they play, as far as we can tell from the recordings, very expansively and very emotionally because they have been taught by pupils of the great composers themselves. This tradition of emotional intensity and expressiveness in the service of the glory of music is what we are in danger of losing and is what you are preserving. It's absolutely the core, the soul of who you are. But we're in a very sterile culture that does not value the grandeur of emotion.

Seymour: Well, I can confirm that. I remember a prodigy in Juilliard. Her teacher knew that I was also working with her and approved of it. At one lesson I demonstrated a nuance in a Chopin nocturne where the left hand plays slightly before the right. She tried but couldn't do it. And then something occurred to me. I asked her, "Honey, tell me the truth. Does it embarrass you to do that?" She said, "Yes it does."

Andrew: So it embarrassed her to be expressive.

Seymour: It did.

Andrew: This is one of the reasons why you are so antagonistic to the major music schools, isn't it?

Seymour: Well, exactly. Many of the most beautiful nuances in performance embarrass young people. They don't want to reveal their inner world, which is the deepest part of them. Many young people think that it's gushing, and not sophisticated enough. Another pupil compared performing with certain nuances as being nude in front of audiences.

Andrew: As a teacher, how do you help a young person have the courage to express the movements of their soul and heart?

Seymour: Well you see, if I hadn't been a performer, and if I hadn't continued to study music as I do to this day, I would never be able to project to my pupils the real soul of music. The only way to do it is to sound it in front of pupils, and to activate their sensitivities this way. In some cases I succeed, and in other cases, as with the prodigy I mentioned, I can't get through to them. I wonder if that girl will ever go to extremes in expressing herself. There are a lot of pianists and other instrumentalists who have major careers and don't really move you when they play. They're amazing technically, but they don't move you. In short, there are all sorts of prodigies: one might have prodigious ears, "photographic" ears, enabling that person the ability to learn pieces by hearing them performed only once; others might be prodigious technically or have the ability to memorize music in record time. Still others may be deeply sensitive to interpretation. When a musician has all of these functions working in harmony, we have the true genius of which there have been very few in any generation.

Andrew: I think a surprisingly high percentage of the major musicians in the world are brilliant technically but without real heart.

Seymour: I'm afraid that's true. So the really great artists are the ones who do everything.

Andrew: You say that your pupils keep you young. At eighty-eight you're teaching more than ever, and I feel that this is a huge secret that you are trying to communicate to all of us: never stop working, never stop pouring out your gifts, never stop offering your wisdom, because that is what will keep you energetic and passionate and young and vital and vibrant.

Seymour: Of course. Your brain has to be activated.

Andrew: It's not your brain, only. It's the heart that needs to keep loving and pouring out love.

Seymour: Well, I assume that the brain sends messages to the rest of the body, and the emotions are connected to all of this. But in all truth I'm not sure where love and compassion come from. I almost don't care to know so long as I feel the impact of love and compassion and can radiate them out to others. If we don't exercise our brains and our emotional worlds, they begin to atrophy. That's when we die early, without having made our contribution. So I want to go on making a contribution. I feel in many respects I'm just getting at the beginning of it.

Andrew: You're just getting to the beginning at eighty-eight?

Seymour: Yes, I have the feeling in many respects there are little secrets that are suddenly revealed to me through my study and teaching and contemplating. And look at this documentary experience suddenly coming into my life at eighty-six. So whatever message I want to give is not just being given to a master class in New Jersey; it's global now. I can't get over this. It's just amazing to me.

Andrew: I remember during our early conversations we discussed the lack of real interest in classical music at this moment, the potential death of the authentic transmission of the soul and the heart through this greatest of arts. So keeping this tradition alive is a deep passion of yours, isn't it? Because you know that so much is at stake. You know that the great classical tradition carries truths and depths of feelings that will die out unless there are people that are willing to serve those truths.

Seymour: Yes, there are many people serving those truths, and I want to be one of them. And in teaching, I know that my pupils are going to carry on the tradition. For example, all my pupils are related to Beethoven. Do you know how my pupils are related to him?

Andrew: No.

Seymour: Oh, when I tell them, they're in utter awe. They never get over it. Let's say that I have a new pupil, and she is studying a Beethoven sonata. I tell her, "Did you know that you're related to Beethoven?" My pupil is completely befuddled and thinks that I'm joking. And then I go on to explain: "I was the only pupil of Alexander Brailowsky, and I also studied with Clara Husserl, both of whom were pupils of Leschetizky. Leschetizky was a pupil of Czerny, and Czerny was Beethoven's pupil. So Beethoven is your great-great-great-grandfather. Moreover, don't think for a moment that it's by name only that you're related to Beethoven. The tradition has been handed down through teaching. So I know things and have read things that Beethoven told Czerny. We would never know certain things about Beethoven if Czerny didn't write them down and pass them on to Leschetizky, and now it's passed on to

Brailowsky and to me. Now I'm passing it on to you. That's how the tradition works." My pupil is deeply impressed to know of the tradition she is now part of.

Andrew: A tradition is a chain of intimacy, isn't it?

Seymour: Absolutely, it is. For example, a fermata is a musical notational sign that means to hold a note or a chord longer than its value. So Beethoven told Czerny, "Every time I write a fermata in my music, always make a ritard before it. Never come to a sudden halt." Well, that goes for all of music, not just with Beethoven.

Andrew: When you are encouraging a person's gifts as a teacher, there's a very difficult line to draw between really wanting to encourage someone's particular subjective gifts and helping them to see that the tradition has impersonal laws and rigors which need to be obeyed.

Seymour: Absolutely.

Andrew: How do you walk that dangerous line?

Seymour: It's not dangerous, it's just part of your musical discipline. I tell my pupils that to disregard a composer's indication of a dynamic or a tempo change is like playing a wrong note. If Beethoven writes "tenuto," which means to hold back the tempo, and you disregard holding back the tempo, you might as well be playing wrong notes. That's how sinful it is. I make them aware of it; I appeal to their conscience.

Andrew: My teacher of poetry, W. H. Auden, said that there were three kinds of poets.

Seymour: You studied with W. H. Auden?

Andrew: Yes. And it was an amazing experience. He would read my poems again and again with the kind of respect due to a Yeats or Rilke, then cut out almost everything in them, sometimes leaving only half a line. He exuded a sad, stoical wisdom and a kindness that sprang, I think, from a brutal experience of loss and loneliness. Auden said there were three kinds of poets: brilliant, authentic, and great. He said many can be brilliant; you can learn how to be brilliant if you have a certain level of intelligence. Then it takes real courage and intensity of being to become authentic. But very few can make the transition from authentic to great because that depends on mysterious inner qualities, which cannot be reproduced.

Seymour: I believe you can say that about all people in all fields.

Andrew: Indeed, and now here's a question I've been dying to ask you: If I wanted to truly perform Bach, whose playing would I listen to? If I wanted to perform Chopin, who would you advise me to listen to?

Seymour: You're not going to like my answer. I take it that you are the one who wants to experience these composers, right?

Andrew: Yes?

Seymour: Just for clarity, you want to know what pianists you should listen to so that you will understand the music of the composers you are interested in. Is that right?

Andrew: Yes, exactly.

Seymour: Do me a favor, Andrew, and don't listen to any recordings at all. What I'm about to suggest presupposes that you can read music. The ability to sight-read is one of the most important skills in studying music. Now choose a composition you want to understand. Open your heart to it. Be like the film in a camera. Don't have any preconceptions. Allow the sound of the music to fall upon your ear and inspire emotional responses that belong to you alone, just as light does when it falls upon the film in a camera. That's the way the composers' messages will get to you. You will never get it by listening to anyone else. You will then resort to copying someone else's responses to music. There is yet another danger when you listen to the finished performance: it may actually defeat you. You would be justified in saying, "How am I ever going to learn to play on that level?" Believe me, Andrew; I'm speaking from personal experience.

Andrew: I love what you're saying.

Seymour: I never listened to anyone's playing. I never owned any recordings to begin with. And all of my friends and colleagues were getting one CD after another. Now of course, we have YouTube, so if a pupil of mine is going to study a piece, they're going to hear twenty performances of it on YouTube, and they're going to imagine that all these people are authority figures, so they're going to copy what they hear.

And then they're going to bring me their piece and I'm going to show them, "What are you doing here? It says just the opposite."

"Oh, well, I heard Pollini play it, and that's what he did," as though Pollini is the authority on how to interpret anything.

See, one can get very distorted notions. So this is what I would advise you to do. Don't listen to anyone's playing.

Just come to your own conclusions and allow the magical language of music to move you until you're bathed in tears. Then you'll know what the music is all about. After you draw your own conclusions, you need to have a mentor to guide you and to steer you in the right direction. A good mentor will draw out whatever is inside of you, or help you to simulate what isn't inside of you. After you earn the right of saying that you have taken your study of the piece as far as you are able, then it's fascinating to listen to how other pianists interpret your piece. That's the way it's done.

2.

MUSIC AND SHADOW

Andrew: Before we come to the end of this conversation, I have a pressing question for you, Seymour. When you look at yourself, what are your shadows, what do you think are your negative traits, what do you work with in yourself?

Seymour: You call them shadows?

Andrew: Shadows.

Seymour: Laziness.

Andrew: Laziness?

Seymour: That's right. I feel that I could do much more. I don't work long enough, and yet I know that I do work many hours. You see me all the time working. For me it's never enough. My ideals go beyond what I actually do. The other shadow is I don't like that I'm overweight. I know how to rectify it, but I lack the courage to forego gorgeous sundaes here in Maine where I have a freezer. In New York City, I don't have a freezer, so I can't have sundaes. So I'm confessing that almost every night here in Maine I make myself a sundae, and I am guilty about it. That's a shadow, right? That's one of my shadows. Otherwise I'm really a very good person. I'm very disciplined, I'm very orderly, and I love people and I only want to help others.

Speaking about being orderly, I am wary about people whose environment is in chaos. I have a strong feeling that as we walk through a chaotic environment, our eyes register chaos and send chaotic signals to our psyche. In short, I feel that chaos registers in our entire being. That's why I fastidiously make up my bed every morning and attend to responsibilities at the moment they are presented to me, such as paying bills, etc. And I never leave dirty dishes in the sink.

Andrew: I wish I could say the same. I have a disciplined mind but I'm naturally untidy. Every year I make a New Year's resolution to change but so far without success. Now I want to ask you a question that many philosophers have pondered deeply over and some writers have written very intensely about and that is the shadow of music. Remember we talked once about *Doctor Faustus*, the novel by Thomas Mann? In that novel Thomas Mann asks us to entertain the possibility that music itself can be a diversion from truth, a seduction away from the exhausting demands of real life and the challenge to act in life from compassion and a passion to see justice done. Plato banned music in his last work, the *Laws*. Kierkegaard attacked art in general for breeding a certain kind of aestheticism, which could mask real action, ethics, and responsibility. In your own understanding of your passion for music, do you ever feel that you are using music to escape life? Is music something that you sometimes hide under to seal yourself off from the world's pain and despair?

Seymour: Well, what you say has occurred to me. I want to preface my answer by repeating the story I told you about depressing the keys of my aunt's piano when I was three. Suddenly, and without knowing anything about philosophy or any other subject for that matter, I knew that this was my destiny. That was an authentic experience. But while I was enthralled with music, and I had to deal with my father, and all the abusive things he did to me, I did consider quite recently that I may have been drawn to music even more so as a refuge from my father. I was safe in an area that he knew nothing about and where he couldn't touch me, or hurt me. It is also possible that the opposite can be true; if I had a wonderful supportive father who acted as a real father to me, would I still be so passionate about music? There's no way to tell, you see.

Andrew: I think you would have been as passionate. But do you feel you have ever used music as a drug, as a way of not feeling the suffering of the planet, of not relating to the terrible injustices and the need to transform them? Isn't there a danger that the beauty of great art can become a narcotic instead of an inspiration to action?

Seymour: Well I never used it as a narcotic. But I must tell you that music served as a savior in many difficult and even life-threatening experiences. I'm thinking especially of the Army.

Andrew: Please talk about that because I feel deeply that your experience of playing music in the middle of the madness, suffering, and horror that is war was a kind of revelation to you.

Seymour: I cannot begin to tell you of the contrasting experiences I had for two years. They ranged from life-threatening experiences to inspirational ones. Let me begin with basic training. Most people had no idea what young men went through during fourteen weeks of infantry training during the Korean War. Well, I was stationed at Fort Dix. My basic training took place in the dead of winter. I don't believe that any soldier since has endured such rigorous, and even brutal, training. I am convinced that the intense mental discipline required to survive countless hours of practicing helped me through the ordeal. After basic training I had my first indication of how music can act as a life-saving force: the captain of special services put me in charge of a movie theater that had an upright piano in the office. He did that so that I would have time to practice.

To my good fortune, I teamed up with violinist Kenneth Gordon who was the assistant concertmaster of the New York Philharmonic. We were both sent to Korea at the same time. We were flown to Seattle, Washington, and herded onto a single-smokestack ship along with three thousand soldiers, including a thousand Canadian soldiers. We slept in the bowels of the ship, two abreast and four deep. It took fourteen days to reach Japan. When I awakened the first morning, I was stricken with the worst case of seasickness imaginable. There were so many guys throwing up in the latrine that there was no way to get into it. As a result, guys regurgitated everywhere, even onto duffel bags. It was a nightmare. In time, almost all the guys adjusted to the rolling ship. But I didn't. Each night I played Liszt's Sixth Hungarian Rhapsody on an upright piano strapped to the wall of a lower chamber on the ship, accompanied Kenneth Gordon, and ran to the upper deck to regurgitate into the Pacific Ocean. Finally, the ship's doctor told me that I was dehydrated and that I had to go to the ship's hospital for an intravenous feeding. I lay in a real bed suffering from intense nausea. "You'll feel fine almost immediately once the intravenous courses through your body," the doctor told me. He jabbed the needle into my arm and left the room. Ten minutes later he returned, and I was even worse than before. Finally, I went into convulsions. I only remember that he pulled the needle out of my arm and injected me with something else. I floated through what appeared to be spirals and into a state of unconsciousness. When I awakened, a chaplain was sitting on the foot of my bed. It seemed that the intravenous bottle was contaminated, and I almost died.

Once in Japan, we boarded another troopship. But this time we were given steel helmets and M1 rifles with which we had trained in basic training. At 5:30 A.M. we filed up on deck as the ship slowly drifted into Inchon Harbor. We were all terrified knowing that we were entering a war-torn country. I remember thinking that preperformance nervousness is nothing compared to this. To make matters worse, it was April 24, 1951, my twenty-fourth birthday.

Although we were in the midst of war, I was very fortunate to escape combat because I was called upon to offer concerts to fighting men just back from the front lines and to exclusive officers' clubs. Kenneth and I gave over one hundred concerts for the UN troops on the front lines. We also performed with the Seoul Philharmonic, and for General James A. Van Fleet and the generals of all the United Nations in General Van Fleet's office in Seoul.

Andrew: What did you learn about music's power in such extreme circumstances?

Seymour: Oh my dear Andrew, music is more powerful than most people realize. Look, there were guys who had never heard a note of classical music. One such guy came up to Kenneth Gordon, who played an arrangement of "Ave Maria" to induce gooseflesh. This guy said to him, "I never heard anything like that in my life. If you stop playing that fiddle I'm going to break it over your head." Some of the boys would come up to us and burst into tears. I can't begin to tell you how moving it was.

Andrew: What do you think the music did for them in these extreme circumstances? After all, these boys were facing death, and you were offering them the music of the great masterpieces of the Western tradition.

Seymour: We were aware that we were facing death. There's something about music that temporarily suspended all that horror. It was really acting out music therapy in the strongest sense.

Andrew: So in a sense what you experienced in Korea is an answer to Plato and to Kierkegaard and those who damn music as a potential seduction away from reality. What you're saying is that in the middle of war's exploding, ghastly reality, music offered another reality, which helped people bear what they had to bear.

Seymour: I'm sure in a certain sense, those philosophers and leaders of countries had to control the citizens they were responsible for. They couldn't allow music to numb them to the reality of what the state required of them. I can see that might make sense. By the way, I remember reading that Plato only banned certain modes in music that he felt led people to undesirable behavior. But at the personal level, living day to day with the horror of war, music was my savior. I think it saved my life.

Andrew: So music never takes on a negative meaning—you wouldn't say there might be unhealthy madness in, say, Mahler's neurotic grandiosity? You never feel that there's an overemphasis on self in some of Beethoven? You don't feel that music can be subtly perverted by personal craziness?

Seymour: Not at all.

Andrew: Does music then exist in its own realm for you?

Seymour: It's a world unto itself. It doesn't mean anything except itself. It doesn't have any reference to the material world at all, even when it's so-called program music. Music might even imitate something, such as Beethoven's use of a flute to imitate a nightingale in the Sixth Symphony. But in the final analysis, that flute solo becomes part of a musical masterpiece that has no correlation to the material world. It ceases to be a nightingale, and simply becomes a musical experience. In short, music means only itself.

Andrew: And that's its saving genius.

Seymour: It's the greatest gift that was given to us by whoever or whatever is responsible for all of life and the universe.

Andrew: You know, dear Seymour, for years I've been collecting a special golden notebook of quotes that express for me the essence of music's mysterious power. Here is my favorite. It comes from Rumi:

> Know that music is the food of those who love;
> Music exalts the soul to realms above;
> Cold ashes glow and latent fires increase;
> We listen and are filled with joy and peace.

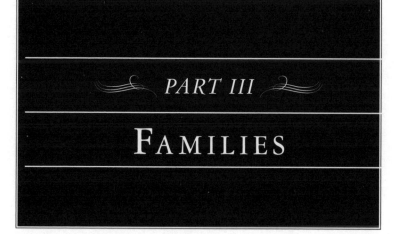

PART III

FAMILIES

1.

To Forgive or
Not to Forgive

Andrew: Seymour, we have been talking about this glorious time in your life—the film, the creativity of it, the excitement of it, and the amazing responses to it. And we've talked about your greatest passion of all, music. Let's shift gears and look into some of the challenges of your life—some of the key early life experiences that shaped you. Let's begin with your relationship with your father.

Seymour: All right, Andrew, but prepare yourself; it's not a pretty picture. From around the age of six, I recall feeling as though a dark cloud was hovering over me. It saddens me to say that this ominous feeling was actually due to the presence of my own father.

He was born in Russia into a family of three brothers and two sisters. He came to this country when he was fifteen. He was brought up in a rough immigrant background. His brothers and sisters were all recent immigrants who did anything they could to survive in their new country, especially when the Depression came and everyone was scrambling. But they were also resourceful and tenacious. They did well in rough businesses like the junk trade, burlap bags, and others. But as for culture, forget it! They never went to a concert or a play; there was just no time or money for frivolities like that. So when it turned out that I was musically and artistically gifted, that was not a source of pride or celebration—at least not at first. It was an embarrassment and an irritant to almost everyone in the generation of my father's social circle.

Like so many fathers, he had a concept of just the kind of a person his son ought to be. But the fact is, I was the antithesis of his concept. The effects of this were blatantly apparent—at least to me: he was morose, severe, and angry in most of his dealings with me. For one thing, he would not tolerate conversation or my boyish joviality with my three sisters at the dinner table. Stern rebukes such as "Stop talking, and eat!" or "Act like a man!" were quite common. When his scolding went unheeded, a hand would fly through the air and slap me, squelching my exuberance and inducing a stomachache, besides.

One evening we had a guest for dinner, a business acquaintance of my father's from Holland. Afterwards we stood around the living room, my father towering over me, and his friend towering over him. It was my father who initiated the discussion—something about my being too sensitive and not manly enough. The Dutchman sized up my ten-year-old frame and arrived at what he thought was a perfect solution: "You should train to be a featherweight boxer," he said to me, his eyes sparkling with a sort of diabolical glee. "You certainly have the physique for it!" I cannot recall my father's reply, but I remember shrinking into the floor in utter horror and embarrassment.

My father arrived home a few days later with a pair of boxing gloves. One glance at them and panic overtook me. It got worse when my brother-in-law Frank fastened them around my wrists and took me outside to the backyard for my first boxing lesson. He jabbed me lightly, to my right shoulder, fully expecting me to retaliate, or at least defend myself. When I did neither, he jabbed me so hard that I was knocked over and burst into tears. As I ran back into the house, I tore off the boxing gloves and threw them onto the floor. Frank didn't comfort or encourage me. I assumed he thought this was a stupid idea on the part of my father. And my father showed no emotion at all. He probably thought that his son was going to be one of those proverbial weaklings. So much for toughening me up.

Andrew: You're very tough, Seymour, but not in the way your father seems to have wanted you to be. It takes incredible mental toughness to practice long hours and work out difficult passages in a musical score, to go on tour and play night after night in concert halls. It's not boxing, but it's very demanding and requires great strength. As a Jew what kind of religious training did your father impose on you?

Seymour: Regarding my religious training, my father had strong ideas about this, too: I was to become a "real Jew"—whatever that meant. When I was six, the same year I began taking piano lessons, a venerable rabbi came to the house to begin tutoring me. With his white beard falling down to his vest, his wide-brimmed hat, and his long black coat, which seemed to touch the floor as he walked, he certainly cut a menacing figure at first. When he spoke, however, his eyes gleamed and his voice revealed a gentle, loving nature. As the lessons progressed, I developed a genuine affection for him, which prompted me, I am sure, to learn my *alef-bet* (the first two letters in the Hebrew alphabet) in record time. Both he and my father were delighted with my progress.

The following year, my father enrolled me in Hebrew school—a major change from the private tutoring. It was adjacent to an orthodox synagogue, which my father attended only once or twice a year during the High Holy Days of Rosh Hashanah and Yom Kippur. The class comprised approximately ten students ranging in age from seven to around fifteen. Lessons lasted from 4 to 5 P.M.— Monday through Friday. It ought to have been a stimulating and productive experience. Yet the course consisted only in teaching us to read and write Hebrew and Yiddish and to recite certain Hebrew prayers from memory.

Andrew: This must have bored you to death!

Seymour: It did. *What* we read or recited seemed inconsequential; we merely parroted the rabbi in a mindless manner. To make matters worse, each year brought with it a new crop of beginning students—and always of disparate ages. This necessitated having to start the course all over again. It was pointless to explain this to my father. As far as he was concerned, I would invent anything at all to avoid going to Hebrew school.

Andrew: But you continued to go, didn't you?

Seymour: I cannot say with what bitterness and resentment I trudged each day to Hebrew school. With the time it took to walk there and return home, in addition to the lesson itself, more than two precious hours were lost to me entirely—hours in which I would have preferred to practice, to work at my various hobbies: building model airplanes, weaving with beads, raising plants, to mention only three, or simply to play out of doors with my friends. Pleadings to my mother were of no avail. She knew better than to oppose my father on religious matters. In the end, it was a question of either going to Hebrew school, or facing my father's wrath.

It did not take very long for me to discover the purpose of this mindless, mechanical instruction: we were to make our fathers proud of us by being able to read any section whatsoever of the High Holy Day prayers at services in the synagogue. I can still hear my father prompting me with "louder, louder!" And I can see him exchanging proud glances with all the men standing around me. I, of course, could only think of the price I had to pay to make my father proud of me. Those were moments when I hated him more than at any other time.

Andrew: I can understand exactly why. You must have suffered greatly.

Seymour: By the time I was nine, I was already wrestling with severe conflicts. On the one hand, my father would brook no discussion concerning Hebrew school: "You'll continue, and that's that!" On the other hand, he seemed bent on erasing the joy and wide-eyed wonder of my childhood. I saw him as a dragon who, when aroused, would consume me in fire. To defy him was unthinkable. Though a dragon, he was still my father, and aren't fathers godlike figures whose every command must be obeyed?

Hide your hatred, I thought, *or certainly that real god up there will find a way to punish you!* I paid a heavy price for repressing my loathing of my father; persistent headaches, stomachaches, and various other neurotic symptoms were some of the consequences I suffered.

Shameful as it sounds, I often wished my father and the rabbis dead. The more I entertained such thoughts, the more guilt-ridden I became. Parents are teachers, and there are even more bad parents than there are bad piano teachers. I spent a good deal of adult life unlearning what my father and several piano teachers taught me. Bad piano teachers can be replaced, of course. But parents and children are biologically chained together. A parent can disown a child, or vice versa, but biology can't be denied.

To put it bluntly, my father and I were stuck with each other. Attending Hebrew school from Monday through Friday was trying enough. But now, my father ordered me to attend services at the synagogue every Saturday morning as well. *Shabbos*, the Jewish Sabbath beginning Friday evening and lasting until sundown on Saturday, was the day reserved for Bar Mitzvah ceremonies. And since my own Bar Mitzvah was a year hence, my father thought I would benefit from watching other boys go through the ritual.

Weekends, of course, were the only days I had free from school. It was a time for music, for creative projects, and for sheer fun. Now, according to my father's new dictum, I would have to spend six days of every week in my least favorite place—the synagogue. A circle of rebellion, which had been slowly building up within me, was now complete. I knew that a violent confrontation was imminent.

Andrew: So what on earth happened?

Seymour: Rabbi Cohen, the chief rabbi of the synagogue, tutored all the boys and girls for their Bar and Bas Mitzvahs. While everything about the school and the synagogue was hateful to me, one aspect of my new training proved to be surprisingly pleasurable. It was the part of the Bar Mitzvah service that called for chanting. All music affected me deeply—whether it was playing my favorite pieces on the piano or intoning the sacred text of the Torah. Since neither the Torah nor the text itself had any significance to me whatsoever, I looked upon the whole experience as merely another opportunity to raise my voice in song. I was doing very well, and the rabbi seemed pleased, when one day I had the misfortune of mispronouncing a word. In an instant, a large gnarled hand shot out across the sacred text and slapped me on the cheek. I remember being more insulted than hurt, and I bit my lower lip to keep from crying. From that moment on, I knew I had two dragons to deal with.

Andrew: Did this make you afraid of older men in general?

Seymour: Yes. In fact I developed a fear of older men, with the exception of my brothers-in-law. For example, I would go on an errand for my mother to the drugstore. It was one of those general stores in which you could buy practically anything. I remember the ice cream counter on one side where you could buy a fudge sundae with real whipped cream for fifteen cents. The proprietor was a charming man and always greeted me with warmth and affection. One look at him, though, and a defensive reaction was set into motion: I tightened up inside, and I would blush for no apparent reason. I had the same reaction in the presence of other proprietors of stores, male teachers in school, and even older male relatives. At nine, I had no notion of what caused those symptoms. Thinking about it now, I believe that I transferred fear of my father to most older men.

Two things helped me shed this neurosis: One was my father's death; the other was the supportive relationship I enjoyed with my brothers-in-law, my surrogate brothers. The attention they lavished upon me compensated for my father's total lack of personal involvement with me. Had it not been for them, I might very well have retained this neurosis throughout my life.

Andrew: Thank God for your brothers-in-law! Now let's return to your Bar Mitzvah. How did it unfold?

Seymour: The day of my Bar Mitzvah arrived. I would imagine that an average boy or girl of thirteen would view that day with a sense of joy and accomplishment. To me, however, it was fraught with as much anxiety as were those later days of important piano recitals.

While most performers are subject to preconcert nerves, even without having had a Bar Mitzvah, I have often wondered whether the sheer panic I felt while standing on that pulpit may, in fact, have contributed to my stage fright as a performer. As far as performing is concerned, musicians can learn to play well in spite of their nervousness simply by taking certain preventative measures. Years of performing experience have taught me about the importance of having tryouts, for example, with one of them being at the concert site, if possible.

But now at my Bar Mitzvah ceremony, an entire year of having been merely an observer proved to be no substitute whatsoever for the real thing, any more than being a member of the audience can prepare a musician for the stage. Imagine, then, suddenly finding myself standing on the pulpit of a synagogue and staring down at the Torah—all for the very first time. And the fact that I was the center of attention in front of my father, mother, three sisters, and an overflowing audience certainly did not help matters any. Only one thought crossed my mind: If I did not do well, if I were to forget any part of the ceremony, it was not god's retribution I feared, but, in a very real sense, that of my father and Rabbi Cohen. The latter stood at my right, appearing more as a threat than a support: "Boinstein, vhat's de matter mit you, Boinstein—are you sick or something?" he muttered in alarm as I began intoning the first of a long series of religious prayers in a barely audible voice. I stood my ground, though, in spite of a pasty mouth, a tight knot in the middle of my stomach, and the rabbi. The ceremony seemed to last forever. It included recitations in Hebrew, chanting from the Torah, and two speeches, one in Yiddish and one in English. In my innocence, I thought that the final words of my speech meant liberation from seven years of my own kind of bondage—a leave-taking at thirteen.

That night, during a celebration dinner at home, my Bar Mitzvah ceremony was quite naturally the chief subject under discussion. In the best of spirits, and with that sense of relief which performers come to know so well, I expressed my happiness at never having to attend Hebrew school again.

With this, my father put down his knife and fork. "What!" he shouted. "You think your Hebrew training is over just because you were Bar Mitzvahed?"

I felt myself grow pale in utter disbelief. That he expected me to continue going to Hebrew school was the very last thing I could have predicted. In an instant, years of repressed rage exploded, and before I knew it, my speaking voice took on all the power which it had lacked on the pulpit: "I'll never go back there, never!" I shouted. "You can punish me, you can say whatever you like, but you'll never make me go back to that school—ever again!"

I thought my father was going to kill me. His fists came crashing down on either side of his dinner plate, sending shock waves the length of the dining room table. His body recoiled against the back of his armchair and the momentum sent him and the chair backwards, spilling him onto the floor.

While my mother and three sisters all rushed to my father's aid, I sat frozen in my seat with only one thought in mind: *I've killed my father!* But he was neither dead nor injured. The chair was righted, and the patriarch, having been helped to his feet, took his seat once again at the head of the table.

When some moments had gone by, and my father seemed to have regained his composure, my mother spoke up. As I have said, she never opposed my father on religious matters, but now his stance must have tried her patience to the breaking point: "Seven years, Max—seven years! Why should he continue on in Hebrew school? After all, he's not going to become a rabbi. It's enough. He should have more time to practice, and to be in the fresh air. No more Hebrew school, and that's final!"

My father, still dealing with the humiliation of having tumbled to the floor, must have found the added burden of my mother's protestations too much to handle. Whatever the reason, his temper was entirely defused. And in a meek voice, no longer that of a dragon, he responded quite simply, "All right, all right, Nellie," and went on eating.

Everything changed after that. Conceding to my mother was, in effect, tantamount to acknowledging her control over my destiny. The fact that the dragon was brought to submission ought to have brought me a sense of relief. But it caused my father to erupt even more often and violently, and the cloud grew even darker.

Andrew: How sad and frightening. And I imagine your father had some pretty rigid visions of your future.

Seymour: Since I was the only boy in the family, my father quite naturally looked forward to having me in his business. When I was fourteen, he insisted that I spend the summer working in his junkyard. I found it abhorrent, and no doubt my feelings were written all over my face. This, of course, did nothing to improve our relationship. As the summer months wore on, my father grew ever more irritable in all of his dealings with me. I particularly dreaded the times when we were alone, such as during coffee breaks and lunches. Then, the silence between us merely heightened the tension that already existed. If anything good came out of my brief encounter with the scrap-metal business, it was that my passion for music and my resolve to make it my life's work grew stronger than ever. It proved how opposition can strengthen one's resolve. In fact I have always thought that my father's total disinterest in my musical ambitions made me practice all the harder.

My parents would have enjoyed an ideal relationship had it not been for me. From the time of the chair-falling incident on the day of my Bar Mitzvah, my mother opposed my father on almost all issues where I was concerned. She knew that practicing was a vital part of my life, and she let my father and everyone else in the family know that my need to practice had to take precedence over everything else. I marvel to this day how she managed to maintain a balance between her devotion to me and her obligations to my father and sisters.

Everything seemed to be going smoothly until one spring night when I was fifteen. My father approached me about working again in his junkyard that summer. Fortunately, my mother was not far away, and she announced to my father, "He's going to practice during the summer, so forget about him working for you or for anyone else—and that's that!"

My father didn't take that too lightly and he argued this point with my mother: "He ought to be working at something during the summer," as though practicing was not work. "It won't hurt him to learn what life is like outside of the house. Besides, he should be earning some money, like other boys do."

My mother handled his obstinacy in the only way she knew how. When my father returned home from work the following evening, she did not prepare dinner for him. My father had lost ground once again, and all because of his musician son.

At whatever price to his vanity, my father had finally to accept the fact that my destiny lay in music, and not in the junk business. When in my late teens I began winning contests and gaining a modest recognition as a pianist in New Jersey and New York City, his attitude changed considerably.

Andrew: How exactly did it change?

Seymour: From that point on, he became surprisingly generous in his support of my musical activities. He was not rich, by any means, but there was always money for whatever I needed—the rental of halls, managerial fees, clothing, etc. But even though he went through the motions of supporting me, something within him could never wholeheartedly accept my choice of career. I remained an enigma to him—and him to me. In fact, when he was asked how many children he had, his reply was always the same: "I have three daughters and a pianist!" There was more than irony in his reply. Brought up in a society that frowned upon music as a career for a man, he was deeply distressed that his own son was a musician. Similarly, I was embarrassed to tell my teachers and my musical friends that my father was a junkman. We were both caught up in a hopeless web of incompatibility—to such an extent, in fact, that I can recall only one circumstance in which I was not uncomfortable in my father's presence, and that was when we listened to one particular radio program together.

In spite of all the differences between us, my father and I shared one thing in common—sentimentality. He, more than I, would often weep openly at the slightest provocation. Every Sunday afternoon he and I listened to a radio program entitled *The Greatest Story Ever Told*. It was an ongoing series recounting incidents in the life of Jesus. Listening to a radio program, of course, precludes conversation, and this was no doubt the fundamental reason why it was the only pleasurable thing we ever did together. At any rate, when the voice of Jesus spoke in parables at the end of each half-hour segment, my father sobbed uncontrollably. I, too, was emotionally stirred, and wept along with my father.

Andrew: Why do you think your father wept?

Seymour: If only we had not been strangers to each other, if only I had had more courage, I would have asked him why he wept: Was he secretly drawn to Christianity, or was he simply responding to the significance of the parable? Considering that my father had so little connection with me and my aspirations, I also found it more bizarre than touching that he wept when he listened to me play certain pieces: Was he moved by the music, did he regret his past behavior towards me, or was he finally proud of his son, the pianist?

He is gone, now, and I will never know the answers to these questions. He died of liver cancer in July 1964 at the age of seventy-two. I was thirty-seven. Ironically, my father, so far removed from me in life, died in my arms. Near the end, I was the only person whom he allowed to perform certain hygienic necessities, which he could no longer handle.

It was not until I was around fifty that I was finally able to utter the truth of my feelings: I hated my father. Even today, the mere thought of him evokes a montage of unpleasant images from my childhood.

Andrew: Please share some of them if it's not too painful.

Seymour: He is about to leave the house to go deep-sea fishing with his friends. I plead with him to take me along. He ignores me. I am left with an overwhelming sense of rejection—a theme that repeats itself throughout our relationship.

I see him in the cellar of our home in Newark, determined to teach our full-grown police dog, Scottie, to stand on his hind legs. He holds a large shovel in one hand, and grasps Scottie's collar with the other. But Scottie, like me, cannot satisfy my father's expectations. I can still hear the howls of pain as the shovel comes crashing down repeatedly on Scottie's haunches. My father's sadistic rage is mounting, and I scream, "Stop it! Stop it!" But he ignores me and continues to beat Scottie.

And finally, there are images I can never forget: I am three, perhaps four. I'm with my father in the bathroom of our apartment on Payne Avenue in Newark. He's toilet training me. He is exposing himself. Now I am six. We are alone in the living room on Keer Avenue. I am sitting on his lap on the sofa. He is fondling me. And this went on for two more years. I remember feeling confused and repulsed. But I sat there thinking this is what fathers do to their sons.

I believe my father lived in fear that I remembered these episodes. His general irritability, his attempts to suffocate my nature, and his constant habit of avoiding my glance all seemed to be symptomatic of this. I see his behavior towards me as a protracted psychological shovel beating, a futile attempt on his part to beat down the past in the hope of obliterating it entirely. It was not I, of course, whom he psychologically, and sometimes physically, beat. Rather, I became in his eyes a symbol of guilt for the things he had done to me. He wasn't punishing me or Scottie; he was punishing himself.

Curiously, no one else in the family suspected what had gone on repeatedly between me and my father. They attributed the tension existing between us to my father's disappointment at not having me in his business, and to a general incompatibility. Besides, my father affected a certain normalcy when in the presence of my mother and sisters—a normalcy such as might have existed between any father and son. He even addressed me as "pal" (he pronounced it "pel"), as though he and I were the best of friends. I remember as a child actually wincing at the very sound of that name. If anything, his calling me "pel" merely intensified the emptiness of our relationship.

I am now profoundly saddened to think that I never knew that sweet exchange that can exist between a father and son. Instead, I had to cope daily with my father's neuroses, which he transferred to me through his actions, his words, or simply by the look in his eye. Small wonder, then, that I wept more profusely at his passing than did my mother and sisters—not out of love or affection, by any means, but rather for the father I never had. When I take stock not only of what my father did to me, but also what he deprived me of, there is no way I will forgive him.

Andrew: Seymour, how dreadful to think that this was going on during one of the most impressionable periods of your life. But see how you have survived and made such a success of your life. I've listened very carefully to what you've said about your father, and I respect deeply what you have been through, but I do have a different perspective on forgiveness.

Seymour: I would love to hear it. I'm open to change all the time. Are you open to change too?

Andrew: I hope that my whole life is an invitation to change.

Seymour: That's a wonderful statement. Most people could never say that; or if they do say that, they don't act it out.

Andrew: Just as you had a very difficult father, I've had a very difficult mother. Not only did she send me away to boarding school at six, making me feel for most of my life secretly worthless and unlovable and suspicious of love; she also later on attacked my sexuality and creativity in lethal ways that for far too long polluted both. The suffering and the horror that my mother has caused me has really posed the central problem of my life, which has been how to face it and how to forgive her for it. And what I've discovered is the necessity of doing everything I can to forgive her so as to release myself from as much of the pain that she's caused me as I can—and also to live up to my own spiritual ideals that have been formed for me by the Christ and by the Dalai Lama. As I've gone on this journey, I've really chosen three ways of approaching this task. One is that I've plunged into a deep analysis with a brilliant and fierce Jungian, who has made me face the range and extent of my mother's madness and her destructiveness, which I was until my early fifties largely in denial about. The second way of healing has been to explore my mother's life and the terms of my mother's own psyche and temperament so as to be able to understand why she has acted as she has acted.

Seymour: Did you succeed in understanding why she acted like that?

Andrew: Yes, I did. For twenty years now, I've spent hour after hour talking to her about her childhood, her relationship with her mother, her early dreams and what happened to her as a young woman. What I've realized from what she's told me is that she could not have acted in any different way, and this has been a source of acceptance for me and of compassion for her. Her mother—the concert pianist I've spoken about—was bitterly jealous of her exuberance and beauty and also the love my grandfather showered her with. My grandmother, who had a psychotic temper, took it out on her daughter, left her mostly in the charge of a nanny who beat her with a hairbrush, terrified her continually, and threatened to kill her if she told anyone.

My mother dreamed all her childhood of becoming an actress and defied her parents by actually doing so (they wanted her to become a respectable secretary and marry a rich businessman). Then, at nineteen, she scuttled her growing career in musical theater by singing when she had

a bad cold and permanently ruining what had been a soar-
ing, strong soprano. Because of her generation's paranoid
rejection of analysis as only for the crazy, she has never
been able to either understand or integrate the shattering
that these appalling experiences inflicted on her. For fifty
years she's been a high-functioning alcoholic with multiple personalities, some of them truly terrifying.

The third perspective that I've really cultivated is the
perspective of seeing what she did to me in terms of the
whole meaning and unfolding of my life. Just as perhaps
without your father you never would have dived into music
as an oasis of refuge, so without the pain that my mother
caused me, I don't think I would have gone on such a spiritual journey to discover the feminine that I needed so
deeply, and I don't think that I would have plunged into
my creativity as a way of saving my life with quite such
intensity. So seeing my life and her role in it from that
perspective, there is a way in which I need to kneel in gratitude to my mother and bless her for the gifts she has inadvertently given me.

When I was in Australia recently, the Dalai Lama made
us all laugh very much by saying, "I am so grateful to the
Chinese because they have made me, without meaning
to, the most popular Dalai Lama in history." My mother
didn't mean to create my passion for the divine and she
didn't mean to reinforce at a primordial depth my hunger to create, but the result of what she did to me did all
of those things. So with those three perspectives, a deep
facing of what really has happened, a deep commitment to
understand why she has been the way she has been, and a
commitment to see my life in a larger and more universal
perspective, I'm finding as I grow older that I can forgive
her more and more and that I can slowly release myself

from the suffering and outrage and savage anger that I've had for so long.

Seymour: May I ask you a question?

Andrew: Yes.

Seymour: What is the real essence of the word *forgiveness* here? Does your forgiveness have any effect upon your mother, or does the act of achieving forgiveness only free you of retaining anger and resentment towards her?

Andrew: I believe it has affected my mother.

Seymour: And how does it affect her?

Andrew: I think that when there's such a close relationship as mother and son, the mother subconsciously knows that her son may not have forgiven her, or harbors real resentment and rage secretly, however skillfully he may think he deals with them. And when truly I have forgiven her, I'm sure that her psyche will register that at the most profound level and that will be healing for her. She's now eighty-eight and disintegrating into Alzheimer's, but there are already tiny signs in our recent conversation that this is so. Just the other day, she said, for instance, for the first time, "You're a lovely son. I love you. I know you love me." She said this very fast and with the most un-English sob in her voice. You can imagine how those words moved me. After she hung up, I found myself looking at the receiver in my hand as if it had turned to gold. I pray every day that before she dies, we will be at peace with each other. My analyst tells me that this is a sad fantasy and it may well be, but I am holding out for a miracle. I also think that—and this comes from my belief in what the Hindus call "karma," that what we do returns to us in the form of fate—that really forgiving my mother will also heal her at deep levels. So forgiving her, I believe, will release and help speed her on her long journey towards liberation.

Your father, Seymour, died when you were in your early thirties. I'm sixty-three; my mother is still alive. For me the fact that she's still alive is a mixed blessing—a blessing because we both still have time to change and transform, and a mixed blessing because the wounds she inflicted on my whole being are still bleeding, and she is still—though far less often than before—saying and doing things that sting them open.

Seymour: You and I discussed that perhaps we drew more deeply to our passions, you to spiritual interests and me to music, as a refuge from our parents. I never said it was a fact. I said, "It's possible." So here's the bottom line: you can't be sure that you went ever deeper into your spiritual searching and knowledge, and similarly I can't be sure that I practiced even harder because my father abused me and sent me to Hebrew school.

Andrew: While it may be supposition, it is as life has turned out. And I think there's a realism about it.

Seymour: Well, but life might have turned out positively for us even if your mother was an angel and my father never abused me or forced me to go to Hebrew school for six years.

Andrew: It might, but it didn't.

Seymour: But we can't tell, can we? There's no way to tell.

Andrew: I find it very intriguing that you made a decision not to forgive your father, but to exclude him from the depths of your life. And you accomplished this through the practice that you do of being surrounded by what you so beautifully described in the film as a crystal translucent dome which keeps you safe from the dark and destructive in your life.

Seymour: Yes. You know what sublimation means, when you push things away? What our parents did to us is symbolic of a scar on our psyche. It will never go away. That scar is there forever. I tried to heal that scar by purposely not sublimating what my father did to me. In other words, by not pushing the memory of it into my unconscious where it would have continued to harm me subconsciously. The result would have been ulcers, a stroke, or even my early death. In short, when you suppress evil, it goes on working in your psyche.

Here is my observation of what you told me about the problems with your mother: I fear that you might have wasted a lot of time in trying to get rid of the scar through forgiveness because you will never get rid of it. I believe that the only reason I don't suffer any scars from my father is because I can still keep my eye on him through my translucent dome. I no longer feel any psychological injury at all from what he did, and I have no conscience whatsoever in saying that I hated him. That is a fact. I'm not pretending, and I can't change it. I really hated him for those sexual incidents I mentioned earlier, and for forcing me to go to Hebrew school. I hated him and I never will take that back. I created my translucent dome because I refuse to sublimate what he did to me. Rather I want to keep my eye on it and on him, thereby shifting control for my destiny away from my father and into my own two hands.

Andrew: That's fascinating.

Seymour: I love my image of the translucent dome. It's helped me a lot. Now please forgive me for even suggesting this, but I wonder if therapy and researching why your mother did those things to you might have been the wrong approach in dealing with the problem.

Andrew: Well, I don't feel that because, first of all, I have never felt that the scars would go away. I never tried to ignore them, and I've known from my experience of myself that the pain that was caused will be with me until the end of my life. What I wanted was not to be destroyed and dismembered by it, not to be rendered suicidal about it, not to be unconscious of its effects on me.

Seymour: So you too tried to objectify it, to keep it away from you in whatever way you can.

Andrew: Yes, to see it, to be clear about it.

Seymour: And did that happen?

Andrew: Yes.

Seymour: Ahhh, then I'm happy for you.

Andrew: What also has happened is that through really making an effort to understand her life and where she's come from, I've come to appreciate her and see the places in her which are deeply brave and imaginative and loyal; and that has given me love for her which I perhaps could never have had if I had just stayed with my own experience.

Seymour: Did you tell her what she did to you?

Andrew: No, she would not be able to hear it. She's constructed for herself an idyllic biography which has almost no relationship with reality.

And she's disintegrating in Alzheimer's, so she's psychologically and spiritually incapable of confronting anything that differs from her fantasy about her epic, wonderful life.

Seymour: How very sad. But how can you love her after what she's done to you?

Andrew: I find I can and I don't know how I can.

Seymour: What form does that love take?

Andrew: Concern for her, prayer for her, deep delight when she's happy; real worrying about her circumstances and doing anything I can to alleviate them.

Seymour: I have an important question to ask you. Do you really believe what you told me, or is it possible that you are acting out of a sense of obligation rather than a real feeling of love and forgiveness?

Andrew: I didn't go on my journey of forgiveness out of duty. I knew I had to do it to get to a different level of sanity and awareness and spiritual evolution. It was a choice that I made for myself.

Seymour: Were you influenced by what the Dalai Lama taught you about forgiveness?

Andrew: I've been influenced by everything I've ever read about forgiveness because the teachings on forgiveness come from the highest place in the human soul. Forgiveness is the crown jewel of all of the enlightenment systems. It wasn't simply His Holiness or Jesus, it was also my experience of people in my own life who have achieved great freedoms through forgiveness, who had been through horrific things but who had managed to clear themselves inwardly by forgiving the people who had done such terrible things to them.

Seymour, I think you and I would both agree that what happened to the Jews in the concentration camps is the greatest single crime in human history and an example of almost unimaginable evil and brutality. Yet I have to tell you that I have had the honor of meeting several people from the camps who had truly forgiven their captors and through their heroic choice of forgiveness had been released from a great deal of suffering. I knew people, too, who had fought against the British in India but who had truly adopted Gandhi's inner separation between the crime and the criminal and had been released by that. So, I've had many examples of people in my life who have achieved great spiritual depth through consciously going on a journey towards forgiveness.

Seymour: My question is: Would not greatness of heart exist whether or not you've been subject to extreme suffering?

Andrew: Of course it can.

Seymour: Then what is the point of suffering?

Andrew: Very often in our lives, it's through extreme ordeal that we discover and bring to birth the reality of who we are.

Seymour: But what about evil? What was done to each of us by my father and your mother is evil, and I would say that your mother and my father will never change. They are victims of brain damage. As such, they lack a basic conscience, even though glimpses of a conscience may appear occasionally. But if we lived with them all over again, they would do the same things to us. There's an evil going on inside.

Andrew: Can I ask you a question from a different perspective: What qualities did you inherit from your father that you recognize?

Seymour: None.

Andrew: You have nothing of your father inside you.

Seymour: Absolutely nothing.

Andrew: Really?

Seymour: I have all the qualities of my mother. I have no masculine qualities from my father. I have to tell you the truth. I was living in a household with a stranger. I had no indications that he was my father. I was terrified of him from the earliest time on.

Andrew: So you don't recognize any of your qualities as coming from him.

Seymour: None. Categorically, none. My mother and my sisters adored him, so there must have been redeeming qualities in him that were never directed at me. You see he disapproved of me from early childhood on.

Andrew: It's interesting because by contrast I have so much from my mother, which is one of the reasons why I so want to be able to forgive her completely.

Seymour: Really?

Andrew: I've inherited her passion, I've inherited her hilarity, I've inherited her gift for language, I've inherited her intuitiveness, I've inherited her sense of drama. I've inherited her looks. So there's a huge amount of me that is like my mother; and one of the reasons why I work to be able to forgive her, truly, is because I am deeply grateful for the qualities that I've inherited from her. I'm very grateful for the gifts that I could only have received through her, through the very person who's caused me the greatest damage and suffering.

Strangely, I've inherited far more from my mother than I did from my father, whom I loved, and who was in many ways a kind and compassionate man of deep dignity; although, of course, I have had to face the damage he passively inflicted through his inability to protect me from my mother's emotional savagery. So I've come to see, Seymour, that from my mother I've not only inherited the central damage and sufferings of my life, but also the gifts that I've pursued and developed to transmute and transform them.

Seymour: Oh, well, dear Andrew, in that case, the whole situation changes drastically.

Andrew: There is a significant difference here because if you truly feel that you've had nothing from your father, that he gave you nothing, then the desolation of that is so extreme that I hear why you wouldn't find him forgivable.

Seymour: Now that you have told me about your mother, my compassion for you quadruples. Because I realize that she had so many wonderful qualities that she transferred to you, and she tried to poison them by the negative aspects of her behavior to take them all away from you. Giving and taking, that's the worst situation. So my deepest compassion to you. You don't have to have compassion for me because my father never took anything away from me. He never gave me anything. I'm free from him. He was like a stranger in my home.

Andrew: Did your father's cruelty and craziness make it hard for you to love yourself? Did you really have to fight to understand yourself, to love yourself?

Seymour: He tried to obliterate everything that was natural and beautiful about me.

Andrew: And you feel there's nothing at all to salvage from your father?

Seymour: Do you know what zero looks like?

Andrew: Yes.

Seymour: Well suppose that a woman lived in your house and told you she was your mother. And she was a complete stranger. How would you feel?

Andrew: Bewildered.

Seymour: That's how it was with my father. He was a male figure walking around. I had no contact with him. No communication with him.

Andrew: Now, Seymour, here's a question. Given that your father was such a negative male in your life, how did you integrate your own masculine?

Seymour: I was so fortunate. Brothers-in-law, three of them, came into my life before I was even twelve. My three sisters were all older than I was.

Andrew: So they married, and they brought into the family three men who truly related to you and loved you; and you could see that they were generous, big-hearted men, successful men, and that they gave you a vision of the masculine.

Seymour: Yes, they did this long before they married my sisters. When I was six, my eldest sister's boyfriend, Frank, came into my life, followed rather quickly by two other brothers-in-law. They courted my sisters, and they included me whenever they went to special restaurants, picnics, and movies. By the time I was twelve, all three brothers-in-law symbolized two important roles in my life: surrogate fathers and older brothers. They bought me all sorts of creative gifts which enabled me to express my creative bent. I can't tell you how grateful I have always been to them.

Andrew: And they loved you back?

Seymour: Oh my dear yes, unconditionally. I was like their mascot. And when I gave my first concert at eighteen in an impressive auditorium in Newark, New Jersey, my three brothers-in-law took care of the ticket sales, and the giving out of the programs. They were so proud of me. And I was so grateful to them.

Andrew: And in them you saw the true masculine, the loving and supportive masculine.

Seymour: Oh, did I ever. Of course. I was saved.

Andrew: Looking at your whole family's history, are there musicians in your family, are there artists in your family? Do you recognize, during the generations, any beings who you feel close to in your family?

Seymour: There was one cousin, Stanley Yeskel. He was the son of my father's sister. So he was a close blood relation. He was a jazz pianist and toured with the biggest bands of the day. He loved to come over and listen to me play. His father, my uncle Willie, owned a textile business and had millions of dollars. Uncle Willie refused to allow his son to continue to play the piano. He forced him to be part of his textile business. So Stanley stopped playing the piano, and was miserable ever after.

One Sunday, Uncle Willie and his wife, Aunt Tillie, visited us in my parents' Newark, New Jersey, apartment. We all sat in our living room. I was fifteen at the time. Uncle

Willie started the conversation: "So, Sonny ("Sonny" was my family name), how's it going with your piano?"

"I'm practicing a lot, Uncle Willie."

"Sonny, why don't you give up this silly dream? Chopin should've been buried with his music. You're not going to make any money doing this, you know. Your father has a good business. Go into business with your father. You'll make a nice living, you'll find a nice Jewish girl, you'll get married and raise a nice family. You know, you're not going to have any friends if you're poor. Nobody's going to want to be your friend."

My father turned pale. Finally Uncle Willie finished his diatribe against me and my future.

I calmly inquired, "Have you finished, Uncle Willie?"

"Yep! You can say whatever you like."

I remember staring at him with dagger eyes and saying, "Uncle Willie, it is you who are the poorest person I know. You have no sensitivity for beauty, you've never been inside a museum, and the only concert you ever attended was mine, and that's because your wife dragged you to it out of shame."

I thought my father was going to have a heart attack.

Andrew: There's something in you so strongly, passionately turned towards art.

Seymour: All true, Andrew. The more my father or anyone else opposed me, the more resolute I became. The more my father slapped me to "be a man," the more I inwardly opposed him and thought that he would never beat the child out of me. Now, where does that come from? As you know, children often cower under such treatment. They get beaten down and can't survive. I don't know what helped me to survive. I can't account for it. I have a hunch that my *spiritual reservoir* was overflowing at birth. It kept reminding me that I had to fulfill a mission in life. I always knew that the mission would be fulfilled through music.

2.

The Divine
and Not So
Divine Feminine

Andrew: It seems like a miracle to me that you were able to hold on to your sensitivity and artistic desires in the face of your father's efforts to make you a "man." The turning point in your life had to be when your mother stood up to him—took charge—and gave you the undying support to become a musician and an independent individual and artist. Tell me about your mother.

Seymour: Her maiden name was Nellie Haberman. She was born in Warsaw, Poland, and came here when she was three. I really don't think I would have turned out to be the person that I am without my mother. She was my lifeline to everything. It had been a total patriarchy until I was Bar Mitzvahed and my mother stood up to my father and said, "Enough, Max, it's enough." When my father uttered the phrase "All right, Nellie," that was the end of his domination over me. She took over and protected me. And as for me, I mostly played the obedient son to my father to avoid outward conflicts with him as long as he was alive. She knew that I was going to be a musician, and she did everything possible to help me.

Andrew: Did you always love her?

Seymour: I loved her dearly, even when she spanked me. She was a wonderful cook and a baker. One of her specialties was butter küchen, including rugelach, all made out of yeast dough. The supply vanished in no time at all, but my mother always stashed away six pieces in a secret place for her *zeenala* ("little son"). I had three older sisters, you know. My sisters knew about it, but they never resented it. They accepted the fact that I was her favorite child.

I would sometimes ask my mother, "Am I your favorite child?"

"No, no," she protested, "I love all my children the same!" But in truth, I was her only son, and the only one fortunate enough to be gifted. She loved me best of all.

Andrew: Tell me more about her.

Seymour Well, she had no formal education, but she was as wise as a philosopher. She had the capacity for unconditional love. When she loved someone, she would go to any length to protect them. She would protect me even at the expense of her own comfort or desires. So when I lived in New York City, and my father died, I taught in my mother's apartment in Millburn, New Jersey, twice a week specifically to keep her company. She would prepare lunch and usually cook dinner for me. When my pupils came into the apartment and smelled the aromas coming from the kitchen, my mother would take them into the kitchen and give them a spoonful of the gravy from the simmering pot on the stove. My pupils adored her, and she them.

Now it came to wintertime. Often there were blizzards on the day of my teaching in New Jersey. The phone would ring: "You're not coming in," this, in spite of the fact that my mother lived to see me twice a week.

"Mama, I am coming in."

"Do you want to make me sick?" she retorted. "You're not coming in, and that's that!"

"All right, Mama, I'm not coming in!"

She had all my pupils' phone numbers, so she could call them. My pupils told me exactly how my mother handled the lesson cancellations. Their phones would ring, and they would pick up the receiver and say, "Hello," whereupon they heard only one word: "Cancelled!" That was all my mother said, and then hung up.

She was also very funny. One incident in particular remains in my memory. I accompanied her to Israel on her seventy-fifth birthday. On the day of our departure, we were two of four hundred passengers on an El Al jet. Midway on our flight to Israel, my mother looked around at the crowded plane. It was unusually quiet when she suddenly blurted out, "Oh my God, I have never seen so many Jews in one place." It seemed as though the entire plane went into hysterics at my mother's remark.

I adored her. When she was dying at ninety-two (I was sixty-two), I really wanted to die with her. I lived in the hospice with her for ten days while she lay in a coma. The attendants set up a cot next to her bed. I only left the room to get meals. On the tenth day, the nurse placed a stethoscope to my mother's chest, and without a word placed my mother's hand into mine. "She's going," the nurse told me. I held my mother's hand as she left this earth.

I couldn't believe how deeply I felt about her passing. Even years later, just saying the word *mother* would cause a constriction in my chest. To cite one example of how long my sense of grief lasted, twelve years after her passing, I went to a restaurant with a violinist friend. I ordered a lamb shank. When the waiter placed it in front of me, I said to my friend, "This was one of my mother's specialties," and I started to sob uncontrollably. It took me completely by surprise.

Andrew: When you say you wouldn't be who you are without her, what do you really mean? What in her lives in you, what did she give you that has enabled you to live your life? What are the ways that you and she are alike?

Seymour: I would say that it wasn't only what she gave to me. It was also what I knew I was giving to her. We adored each other. I kept her up by visiting her, and she kept me up as much as she could. When I moved to New York City, she knew that I was in financial need. Being new to the city, I didn't have enough pupils to pay the rent. Every week she filled two huge shopping bags with every conceivable food imaginable, took a bus into the Port Authority Bus Terminal in New York City and took a taxi to my apartment. On the way out, she would slip a twenty-dollar bill into my hands. In those days, twenty dollars went a long way.

She was very proud of me. It's such a pity that she didn't live to see this documentary. Whenever I took her to an engagement, people would surround her and ask questions about me, such as "What was he like at home? Did he practice a great deal? Did he struggle to get engagements?" My mother's answer to the last question was always the same: "They threw him out the front door, and he'd come in the back door." That was her favorite phrase, and mine, too.

As a matter of fact, she was filled with phrases. Some of them were in Yiddish. Mother would toss them out to my sisters and me. When phrases were in Yiddish, we would surmise its meaning by the situation. For example, in situations where one might want to say, "So what else is new?" Mother would come out with "*A bletel zum opsis.*" Finally, around the age of fifty, I asked my mother, "Exactly what do those words mean? What is a *bletel*, for example?" I was charmed by what she told me. Evidently, shoes in the old country were made exclusively of leather. There were no rubber heels or soles. So the literal translation of *a bletel zum opsis* is "So there's leather on your heel." In other words, "So what else is new?"

As I said earlier, mother was a natural philosopher. When I moved into my home in Maine in partnership with a friend to share the expenses, I would occasionally relate problems that arose between us, petty things like the time I replaced the cream cheese in the refrigerator on the third shelf instead of the second where it had been. When my mother heard this story, she responded with "My son, there's no house large enough for two people." On another occasion, we met a couple where the woman was a loud, aggressive shrew, and the husband a meek, introverted character. I said to my mother, "How can that man live with a woman like that?" My mother had the perfect explanation: "My son, don't you know that every pot finds its cover?" She was filled with little nuggets of wisdom like that.

Andrew: I think when I listen to you that you were deeply affirmed by your mother. Whatever happened to you, and whatever you suffered, you knew that there was one person who absolutely accepted and loved you. And in this you were blessed. No one in my family has understood or supported my work or life. This caused me anguish until, on my fiftieth birthday, I made the decision to accept it, the inevitable limitations it has imposed both on my evolution, and often on my trust in life.

Seymour: Oh, Andrew, I am so sorry for what you have suffered. Yes, in my case, you're right: I was blessed. My mother loved me absolutely and unconditionally.

Andrew: And this unconditional love that you experienced from your mother gave you a deep self-confidence beneath and beyond anything that you could have experienced on your own. Your mother gave you the greatest gift a mother could give her son.

Seymour: She did, she did. And I reciprocated by being the best son I knew how. Near the end of her life, my mother developed macular degeneration. She was practically blind, and she gave up her apartment in New Jersey. She moved in with my eldest sister in Florida. But it turned into a nightmarish situation. My sister was actually cruel to her. According to my mother, she was left alone far too often. And on one occasion, my sister called my mother into the kitchen for lunch. My mother asked for something in particular and my sister screamed at her and told her she would have to eat what had been prepared for her. None of us could believe these stories. But evidently my sister found it too stressful to care for our mother. Concerning this, my mother interjected another bit of wisdom: "My son, a mother can take care of twelve children, but twelve children can't take care of one mother."

I was in Maine when she told me of her deplorable problems in Florida. I was in the middle of writing a major book called *Twenty Lessons in Keyboard Choreography*. It occupied around ten years of my life to write. I put it all aside and flew to Florida to rescue my mother from my sister. We then flew together to Portland, Maine, where I had my car parked, and I drove my mother to this home. I had brought all her bedroom furniture to this house when she moved out, and she was thrilled to be reunited with her bed again and all the relics of her former bedroom. I cooked her favorite food. I thought that this was the end of my creative spell of writing that book. But I couldn't have been more mistaken. My mother sat in an upholstered chair in my studio covered in a blanket, while I worked away at the piano improvising and writing my book. From time to time I would wail, "I don't know how to go on," whereupon my mother, who sat quietly for hours, responded with "Don't worry, my son. You'll find a way to do it." She sat there, encouraging me on, never demanding anything from me, just bathing in the glory of her creative son.

At this point, Andrew, I have to confess something about my creative world. As you know I have a compulsion to compose and create. That was a major reason why I quit my performing career. Curiously, nothing makes me more miserable than the process of creating itself; and nothing makes me happier than the final results. It's as though I put up with the process for the reward of completing something. The fact is, creative talent is autonomous, namely, it has a life of its own. So when I begin a composition or a writing project, they demand fulfillment. If I rebel, then I become miserable and guilt-ridden. Therefore whether I want to or not, I have to bring my creative projects to a close.

I brought my mother back to Florida a month later when we had found a beautiful assisted-living home, where she spent her remaining days. Her doctor suggested that she have a cataract removed from the eye from which she couldn't even see light, and behold, my mother had perfect vision in that one eye. She saw all the people in the retirement home where she was living. She saw the flowers I sent her. And she was able to watch TV again. Two months later, she developed heart failure and died.

Andrew: And when your mother died, what did you feel?

Seymour: I wanted to die with her. I couldn't bear to be without her. But I'm a very strong person, and I knew I was going to go on living. There's something most interesting that I forgot to tell you, something concerning my father's death. Right after his death, I went on a purge of some people I knew. I terminated one so-called friendship after another.

Andrew: When your father died you celebrated that in a way by purifying your life of all the false relationships.

Seymour: I did; you said it perfectly.

Andrew: Tell me about how you came back to life after wanting to die with your mother.

Seymour: My music was my salvation, not only then, but also throughout my life.

Andrew: Was your mother also your salvation?

Seymour: In a way, yes. My mother played a powerful role in my life just as music did.

Andrew: And isn't it wonderful that she so loved you as a musician, that she blessed you as a musician?

Seymour: Her son and music were synonymous.

Andrew: But not only were you and music synonymous, she really was brave and wise enough to protect you at crucial moments, as you so vividly described, so that you could unify yourself with your music, so that you could practice, so that you could feel blessed in this very unusual choice given your social background as the son of a Jewish junkman in New Jersey.

Seymour: Absolutely.

Andrew: So here was a mother who could easily have loved you, and even loved your musical abilities, but she did more than that, she protected you in this very unusual choice. How many other junkmen's sons have chosen classical music as their profession? She had great spiritual imagination, she had great imagination of the heart, didn't she?

Seymour: Oh, and how. There are mothers who adore their children, but they're jealous of their involvement in something. It takes away from being involved with the mother. My mother was just the opposite. She would sacrifice her well-being if it meant that I had more time to practice. I'll tell you another example of how protective she was. We lived on the second floor of a two-and-a-half family home. The piano was in the living room adjacent to a den. There was also a dining room, a kitchen, and two bedrooms. My sisters all lived nearby and visited my mother daily. They congregated in the den near where I practiced. After I graduated from high school, I just stayed home and practiced all day and also taught. I refused to go to college. I just wanted to get caught up on neglected disciplines and expand my repertoire. After all, I wanted to be a pianist. The problem was that I heard my sisters and my mother talking throughout my practicing. You know when four women get talking together it can be quite loud. And I was very serious about my playing. Nothing was more crucial than for me to practice without distraction. Finally, one day I had to go into the den and tell them I just couldn't concentrate. To my great relief, my mother took my three sisters into the kitchen and closed the door leading to the living room. From that day on, no one was allowed to enter the living room or den so long as I was practicing. You see, my sisters loved me deeply, and they were also in awe of my talent. So there was never any resentment on their part when my mother took means of protecting me.

Andrew: Have you ever felt from anybody else that degree of protectiveness and love?

Seymour: Not to that extent.

Andrew: What did she believe about God, for example?

Seymour: I never asked her. But she was brought up in a kosher home, and she kept our home kosher, which meant that she bought all her meat from a kosher butcher, and never mixed dairy with meat. For example, if we had a baked potato with meat, we couldn't have butter on it. Chicken fat, yes, but no butter. She had no religious associations whatsoever. She did however go to *Yizkor* services (services for the dead) on Yom Kippur. She went with my father once a year to these services when my father was alive.

When my father died, he had been a member of the temple for twelve years. He was a religious hypocrite while he was alive, for he only went to the temple on Yom Kippur, and spent all day fasting. After he died, we didn't think of renewing his membership in the temple. For after all no one in the family except my father ever went to the temple. But on Yom Kippur after his death, my mother asked me to please take her to the temple for the *Yizkor* service. We were confronted with a long table at the entrance where approximately eight men were sitting. There was also a policeman on duty. I approached the first man I saw and told him, "My father was a member of the temple for twelve years and we haven't renewed his membership after he died. My mother wants to say *Yizkor* for him. Can we please go in?"

"You can't go in without a ticket!" the man said.

I felt a rage swell up within me. "Are you barring my mother from going into the temple?"

"You can't go in without a ticket," he repeated.

At this, I took hold of the table and hurled it across the entrance. The policeman came over to me to restrain me, and people came pouring out of the temple wondering what all the commotion was about. It's totally unlike me to lose my cool like that. But you see it was the result of a pent-up rage against my father for having forced me to go to Hebrew school. And what is the result of six years of

Hebrew school? They won't even allow my mother to say a prayer for my dead father. I just lost it.

A man came rushing over to my mother. He owned the supermarket where my mother shopped. "Mrs. Bernstein," he said tenderly, "come, you'll sit on my seat, and I'll just stay out for a while."

They let her in. A few men reinstated the table. I waited for my mother outside the temple and seriously wondered why I wasn't arrested.

Andrew: As I listen to you speak of your relationship with your mother, I realize she's the source of your mysteries, the spring from which all the streams of you flow.

Seymour: And not only that but my middle sister, whom I help now, the one who's sick, always thought that my mother lived through me. Without me, she thought, my mother would have died long before she did.

Andrew: She stayed alive to be there for you.

Seymour: Only to be there for me, yes. My sister was convinced that my mother lived through me and for me.

Andrew: So you might've been in a certain way her masculine, in the same ways that she was—

Seymour: My feminine. Yes, that's possible.

Andrew: What is the beauty of the feminine for you? You speak about her with such joy in her cooking and her capacity to make a beautiful home, and her loving-kindness and her tolerance. When I say "the feminine in you," and your eyes light up as they do, what qualities do you associate with the feminine through your mother and why do you love them so much?

Seymour: Gentleness, a profound capacity to love beyond the physical.

Andrew: And you feel that the feminine has a much greater capacity for those?

Seymour: Women tend to love for the right reasons. They are attracted to the inner person, and not only how a person looks. I confess that I have always felt that women are superior to men.

Andrew: Why?

Seymour: I have observed the superior way in which they play instruments, and the way they write. We all know that women have for centuries been subjugated. I have a hunch that if they hadn't been subjugated, their capacity and their output would be superior to that of men.

Andrew: Do you think this is one reason why men have subjugated women, because of a deep jealousy of the power and the beauty of what women are capable of?

Seymour: It's possible. I've thought about that.

Andrew: People talk about "penis envy," but I've always thought it was much more likely to be "womb envy," and that men are envious of a woman's capacity to give birth, to have multiple orgasms—this is an astounding power that's in a woman's body and men are jealous of it. Underneath patriarchy's degradation and dismissal of women and the feminine is a terrible secret fear that women actually are far more powerful and creative than men.

Seymour: All possible. Do you feel that they are?

Andrew: Yes.

Seymour: I've never, ever met anyone who agreed with me. You're the first one.

Andrew: I think one of the most wonderful things about our time is that many of the greatest living teachers are women, many of the most powerful writers, really breaking new territory, are women. Many of the greatest and most charismatic singers are women, and now, increasingly, some of the most powerful and transformative politicians are women. I think it's a great privilege to live in an age of the return of the divine feminine.

Seymour: Yes, look at Hillary Clinton.

Andrew: Yes!

Seymour: She may become the first woman President.

Andrew: This gives me hope because I think that what I love about women most is the capacity they have to marry tremendous intelligence and practicality with deep, deep care for people. And if we could have a world in which this kind of power of women was celebrated, and brought into the center, then we'd have a much bigger chance of solving the terrible problems that we are facing.

Seymour: Now, Andrew, I want to tell you a story from my life that shows quite a different view of what impact a woman can have. You won't believe this.

Andrew: That sounds ominous.

Seymour: Wait till you hear. When I was nineteen, relatives of mine told my parents one day that they knew a man who was well connected to the music world. He thought that I was wasting my time staying in Newark, New Jersey, and that he ought to go to a music school in New York City. So my parents met this man, told me of his thoughts, and I agreed. This man arranged an audition at the Mannes Music School and actually escorted me there. David and Clara Mannes and their son, Leopold, were all alive at that time. They ran the school in a private mansion in the East Seventies. It since has moved to a larger building. I auditioned for them. "We'd like to offer you a scholarship," Leopold said after I played for them, "and send you to the most famous teacher in the United States, Madame Isabelle Vengerova. But you'll have to audition for her." I thanked all the Manneses profusely and couldn't wait to tell my mother that I was offered a full scholarship.

I subsequently met some of the students around the school, all of whom thought that Vengerova was a monster. I concluded that they were either stupid or ungifted, which is why Madame was impatient with them. *But she's going to love me,* I thought.

The following week, I went to Madame Vengerova's studio in the West Nineties to audition for her. There were two Steinways in her studio side by side. She sat at one, and I at the other.

"Mr. Mannes has spoken very highly of you," she said. "Please, play for me."

A monster? On the contrary. She was as sweet as any-one could be. I played her a Chopin Nocturne.

"*Mnn,* your wrists are so relaxed," she said. "I have so much trouble relaxing my pupils' wrists! Where did you study to play so beautifully?"

I said, "In Newark, New Jersey."

"Really? How many brothers and sisters do you have?"

I thought to myself, *She's like my grandmother. I adore her.*

She then asked me to play something else; I did. Per-haps it was audacious of me at nineteen, but I asked her if she had studied with Leschetizky.

"*Mnn,* no, my dear, I studied with Esipova, Leschetizky's second wife," she said. "How did you know that I was connected to Leschetizky?"

"My teacher in Newark was a Leschetizky pupil," I told her.

Madame's next pupil was already knocking at the door. "Please tell Mr. Mannes that it will be a pleasure for me to teach you. Please come for your lesson in September." It was June at the time, and she assigned me a day and a time for my first lesson.

Needless to say I practiced harder than ever as the day of my first lesson drew near. I took the train into New York City and couldn't wait to be with my new teacher for my first lesson. I rang the bell to Madame's apartment and was greeted by her servant, who asked me to wait in the foyer. I had settled in a chair for some five minutes when I heard muffled voices issuing from the studio. Then, suddenly, the door burst open, and a tall, attractive young woman came rushing out with tears streaming down her cheeks. As she passed me, she glanced sideways in utter embarrass-ment and was out the front door in a flash.

Before this incident had fully registered upon me, I heard Madame's voice emanating from the studio: "*Mnn,* please come in!" It was more of a command than an invitation. Considering the stern tone of her voice and the sight of her pupil rushing past me in tears, I was understandably apprehensive of Madame's mood. Least of all was I inclined to plant a kiss on her cheek. Madame extended her hand and asked, "Did you have a good summer?"

"Yes, I did. Thank you."

Clearly, there was a tempest brewing beneath her affected charm. She lost no time in beginning the lesson. "What repertoire did you work on since I last saw you?" I mentioned the Chromatic Fantasy and Fugue by Bach and the *Emperor* Concerto by Beethoven. I was about to mention some five other works, which I had prepared for her, but she cut me off abruptly with "*Mnn*, play the Bach for me."

By that time in my life, I was no stranger to various degrees of nervousness, ranging from mild anxiety to utter panic. But the contained cyclone within Madame, plus the scene I had just witnessed, conspired to induce the worst anxiety I had ever experienced. As I began the Bach, I had the distinct impression that my fingers were encased in a block of cement. It took all of my determination to articulate the opening passage. I was much relieved when Madame stopped me almost at once: "Now the Beethoven!" I barely finished the introduction of the concerto when she stopped me again: "Good. Now we will begin the lesson."

With this, she looked at me so menacingly that I felt my shoulders rise towards my ears.

"*Mnn*, tell me, how do you practice?"

No one ever asked me that before, so I thought awhile and replied, "I think it depends on what I'm practicing." I thought that was a very good answer.

Madame suddenly shot me a piercing look and asked in a threatening voice, "*Mnn*, did you go to grammar school?"

I said, "Yes, Madame Vengerova."

"*Mnn*, did you graduate?"

I felt the blood leave my face. "Yes," I replied.

"Did you go to high school and did you graduate?"

"Yes, Madame."

Suddenly she exploded: *"Did not your teachers ever ask you a question before?! Why can't you answer me intelligently?!"*

I turned green and never lost that color for six weeks. She was indeed a monster. She took all of my repertoire away and gave me nothing but wrist exercises. As I think about it now, she had originally complimented me on my flexible wrists. So why did she spend so much time on this part of my playing mechanism? Moreover, she had me undulate my wrist between the fingers and the elbow instead of initiating the movement from my upper arm. As a result, I sprained my wrist. "It's because you carry a heavy briefcase," she ascertained.

At another lesson, she took my hand to simulate a motion. "*Mnn*, why are your hands so cold?" she sneered.

I was terribly embarrassed to tell her the truth, which was that she scared me to death. So I said, "It's very cold outside, Madame."

Never one to lose an opportunity to be sadistic, she replied, "But you've been in this room long enough to be warm."

We're now at the sixth lesson and Madame suddenly inquired, "Why do you look so unhappy?"

I thought, *Well what do you know. The bitch is actually human. I can now confide in her.*

I began very cautiously, "Madame, I know the exercises are very good for me (I hated myself for lying), but I miss playing repertoire. I've lost my desire to practice."

My comment was like a fuse that set off an explosion. She literally screamed, "You fresh, American upstart! You never speak a loud word to me, but your thoughts are fresh! How dare you tell me how to teach you? Why don't you go to (here she mentioned all the piano faculty members at the Mannes School)?! They'll give you nothing but repertoire!" Her tirade continued for minutes. When it subsided, she said, "Did you ever play the B-flat Partita by Bach? Write that down (she always had me keep notes for whatever she said). Did you ever play the first Chopin Impromptu? Write that down. And don't you dare come back next week until every note is from memory."

As I walked out of her apartment, I knew that I would never return. When I entered the elevator, I must have looked frightful, because the elevator man took one look at me and said, "Don't worry, kid, it'll be all right."

When I arrived home, I called Leopold Mannes and told him I will never go into her studio again.

"You can't walk out on Madame Vengerova," he said in a very disturbed voice.

"Then I'm going to give up my scholarship," I replied. "I can't study with a person who thinks that I'm a 'fresh American upstart.'"

He thought a moment and said, "All right, I'll make an exception. I'll send you to another teacher."

I was assigned to Dr. Herman de Grab, who was exactly the opposite of Madame Vengerova. He knew what I had experienced, and was therefore afraid to criticize me for fear of upsetting me.

No sooner did I end my conversation with Leopold Mannes when Irene Rosenberg phoned from Brooklyn. The school registrar gave her my phone number. As I said, she knew what awaited me at my first lesson with Madame Vengerova, and she phoned to apologize for putting Madame in such an irascible mood. While that lesson spelled the end of Madame Vengerova, it was the beginning of one of the longest and most satisfying friendships I ever had, with Irene Rosenberg. She had been studying with Madame Vengerova for six years and admitted to being traumatized by her at every lesson. Inspired by the fact that I left her after only six weeks, Irene decided finally to do the same, thereby forfeiting her graduation from the Mannes School. The following week, the doorbell rang in the Rosenberg home in Brooklyn, and a pupil of Vengerova's handed Irene a box. In it was a ceramic angel that Irene had given Vengerova for Christmas.

Now it's the end of the season, and the school was planning a concerto concert. Four students were chosen, and I was one of them. I was assigned the Bach F-minor Concerto, and Leopold Mannes wrote a cadenza for me. As I walked onto the stage to play, I spotted Madame Vengerova sitting in a box that was practically hanging over the stage. I felt her menacing eyes piercing me. Instead of panicking, I decided to show her what I was really made of. So I tore into the concerto with special verve and played the second movement with deep sensitivity. After the finale, which went brilliantly, I received a standing ovation. You have to forgive me for telling you that I was the star of the evening.

What do you suppose Madame Vengerova did the following morning to retaliate against me for leaving her?

Andrew: What did she do?

Seymour: Would you like to guess?

Andrew: I can't, you tell me.

Seymour: All right, I will tell you. The following morning after the recital, Leopold Mannes phoned me and said that I had to meet him in his office as soon as possible.

Naturally I rushed to New York City. As I entered his office, he gave me a hug and began crying.

"Mr. Mannes," I inquired much concerned, "what has happened?"

He told me that Madame Vengerova phoned him early that day with the following pronouncement: "I will no longer tolerate the gossip that's being spread around, that I'm not good enough to teach that boy. So, either you expel him from the school, or I'll leave the faculty."

"Seymour," he said, still with tears in his eyes, "if she leaves the faculty, the school will fold. She's the key figure here. I have to expel you."

At that point, I started to cry. I loved the school. I loved the intimacy of the classes. For example, there were only six students in the counterpoint class. I was devastated to think of being expelled from the school. I went home to Newark, New Jersey and told my mother.

She said, "What did you do that they expelled you?"

"I played well at the concert," I told her.

It took me about a year to get over that experience. Then I realized what a victory this was. I was an unknown figure from Newark, New Jersey, and yet I was a threat to one of the most important pedagogues in the United States. Many months later, I passed her standing with a group of her pupils in Town Hall, New York City. She looked at me with her piercing eyes as though she was trying to remember who I was.

"Hello, Madame Vengerova," I said. "Don't you remember me? I'm Seymour Bernstein."

"Of course I remember you," she sneered. "You're the boy who couldn't stand me."

She died shortly after that. Though it's sad to say, her death saved other pupils from the poison of her nature.

Andrew: What a story, Seymour. What a classic example of a creative woman who became a monster. Women like that can cause tremendous suffering; they are both manipulative and psychologically brilliant, so they can cause a great deal of destruction, and with a dazzling lack of conscience. It seems to me both the masculine and feminine have disastrous shadows. The masculine, when it's at its best, is noble and generous and clear and filled with energy for duty. At its worst, it's obsessed with power, cruel, harsh, and controlling. The feminine has so many positive qualities, but because of social and political and economic oppression can manifest very great capacities for manipulation and violence, and addiction to power in both blatant and devious ways.

Seymour: The contrast to the other kind of woman is so great that it appears as though they are far worse than negative aspects within men. In my observation of piano teachers, the real monsters are women. There are a few men who are pretty terrible, but not to the degree that women are.

Andrew: What do you think makes this monstrousness in women?

Seymour: They've been subjugated. They've never been given a chance to have major careers.

Andrew: And they take that out on their pupils.

Seymour, I've also been quite intrigued by another important relationship mentioned in the film that you had with an ambiguous, complicated woman who was your patron. Describe a little of that relationship.

Seymour: You mean Mrs. Boos. Strangely enough, I forgot to say in the documentary that I always felt uncomfortable with the name "Boos," since it sounded like "booze." So I called her "Duchess." As it happened, the poet Patricia Benton commissioned me to write some music for her book of poems. She told me that the actress Blanche Yurka was going to recite the poems at Nine East Seventy-Second Street, a mansion owned by a Mrs. Mildred Boos, and would I play the music I wrote during the recitation and then play a group of solos? I was delighted to accept the engagement. And that's how it all started. Mrs. Boos latched on to me at once with invitations to the Philharmonic and the old Metropolitan Opera House where she had first-tier center boxes in both halls. All performances were followed by lavish dinners. This went on for about a year, and one day she told me about her services that she held in her mansion.

"Do you know anyone who plays the organ?" she inquired.

"Well, I can sort of manage the organ. Would you like me to play the organ for your services?"

That did it. You saw in the documentary that as a result of offering to play for her services, I became her favorite person.

Andrew: Right, and then she gave you the keys to her mansion.

Seymour: Yes, she did. I had all my pupils' recitals there, and I tried out my own recitals whenever I wished. It was a five-story mansion with thirty-four rooms. The Duchess also had an estate in Scarsdale with an empty Tudor mansion at one end of it. She gave that to me when I returned from my European debuts, which she sponsored.

Andrew: What happened to your relationship?

Seymour: She constantly made demands upon me.

Andrew: Increasingly demanding.

Seymour: Increasingly, yes. I had to have dinner with her every evening. She had a cook and a servant. It was always formal. I always had to have a jacket on. She had two sons and a daughter. One of the sons was adopted. I would have thought that they would resent me. But all three loved me. They never felt that I was a threat to them. The Duchess showered me with gifts. I remember one Christmas when she made a party for me and asked me to invite eight of my friends. There had to be around thirty presents for me under the tree. I had to open each one in front of my friends. I felt so embarrassed, so ashamed, because I was given all of these luxuries, and they were just as poor as I was. One thing led to another, and when I continued playing the organ for her, she went full blast and paid a manager to manage me.

You heard the rest in the documentary. I eventually felt like a kept man. So one evening I phoned my brother-in-law to pick me up. I left each and every present in the Tudor mansion and returned to my one-and-a-half-room studio in New York City. The poor Duchess had a nervous breakdown. I felt terrible for her, but I could not in good conscience continue to live like that. Her letters arrived, pleading with me to return. I didn't answer any of them. Finally an envelope arrived sealed in wax. She said that it would be easy enough for her to rescind all the legal arrangements she made on my behalf. That was her final ploy to have me return. Quite obviously she was going to leave me a fortune. I refused to answer that letter as well.

Andrew: Did you ever see her again?

Seymour: I visited her every Christmas simply out of allegiance in order to thank her for all the help she gave me. Around five years later, she had several strokes and died.

Andrew: So on the one hand, you have your mother as this marvelous example of the full, all-embracing, all-loving feminine that sustained you and made you who you were, and then on the other hand you have these two contrasting stories about what happens when the feminine becomes crazy.

Seymour: I had another terrible monster teacher when I was quite young, who was almost completely blind. She gave me three free lessons every week, in Newark, New Jersey.

One day, my mother sat me down to have a serious talk with me: "All of Newark is talking about your affair with Louise Curcio." I was shocked to hear this from my mother.

"What are you talking about?" I protested. "I'm not having an affair with her."

She went on with "But everybody knows she has fallen in love with you."

Louise Curcio intended to use me to promote a theory she called "The Dimensional Tone." It was all nonsense, but I didn't know that at the time. She grew terribly demanding. It wasn't long before I broke with her, too.

Andrew: Listening to you, I realize how, over time, you have evolved a healthy relationship with what I'd call the *dark feminine*; you break with its agents as soon as they show their true destructive face. Because of my confusing, tormenting relationship with my mother and my subconscious passion to right and rewrite it, I have very often invited destructive muse-monsters like her into my intimate life. I idealize them and adore them until, usually too late, I find them trying to destroy me, or my work, in the same way my mother has. Even after a decade of fairly brutal analysis, I still find myself sabotaged by a bewildering lack of discernment, which obviously stems from the trauma of my childhood. But I'm slowly becoming wiser, and I promise you, I will learn from you how to be appropriately, even ruthlessly if necessary, self-protective.

Seymour: You must have had wonderful women friends, too?

Andrew: Yes. In the heart of my life, there are a handful of extraordinarily loving, wise, and generous women whom I love deeply and whom I know and feel love me deeply and respect and protect the strange work I'm called to do. Without them, I couldn't be as steadily joyful as I am, or as productive. They are the guardians of my life.

Caroline Myss is one of them. She is not only a great teacher, whose fierce, edgy candor I revere and continue to learn from; she is a beloved, loyal, and passionately generous friend, a soul sister whose hard-won wisdom inspires and hones me. We live just five minutes from each other in Oak Park and call or see each other every day. And then there is Gloria Vanderbilt.

Seymour: You know her? How wonderful.

Andrew: We've been intimate and tender friends for over twenty years now. I met her just after her son Carter committed suicide. She is the Koh-i-Noor, the bird of paradise, of my heart. I never cease to marvel at the extraordinary marriage in her of great, quietly fierce strength and the most poignant and luminous fragility. She's even older than you, dear Seymour, and continues to pour herself out in her art, which becomes more and more brilliant and visionary, and in her astute, kind love for her family and close circle of friends. When I think of the divine feminine in human form, I think of Gloria, still uncannily beautiful at ninety, passionate, tender, brave, determined, creative, endlessly encouraging, and compassionate. To love her and be loved by her is one of the greatest joys and deepest graces of my life. I keep my favorite photo of her by my bed; her wonderful wide smile so aglow with love of life is the last thing I see before I sleep and the first when I wake.

Seymour: Andrew, it is deeply inspiring to hear about these relationships that flourish in reciprocity. Everything that you have said speaks of your profound capacity to love another human being. I'm sure that capacity endears you to all of your friends and students. It certainly endears you to me.

Seymour and Ethan Hawke enjoy a moment of relaxation after the premiere of *Seymour: An Introduction* at the *NYC Film Festival at Lincoln Center*.

Seymour's eldest sister, Lillian, and Seymour, age 2, in a goat cart outside their home in Newark, NJ.

Seymour, age 6.

Seymour's Bar Mitzvah portrait.

Portrait as a soldier during Seymour's
basic training at Fort Dix, NJ.

Seymour making his debut with the *Chicago Symphony Orchestra* in 1968, premiering Villa Lobos' Concerto No. 2.

Foreground: Sylvia (sister)
Front row, left to right: Evelyn (sister), father, mother, and Lillian (sister)
Back row: Saul Armm (brother-in-law), Seymour at 19, and Frank Lozowick (brother-in-law)

Portrait of Seymour's mother
taken in Maine.

Portrait of Sir Clifford Curzon, taken in the Steinway basement.

Clara Husserl (Aunt Clara).

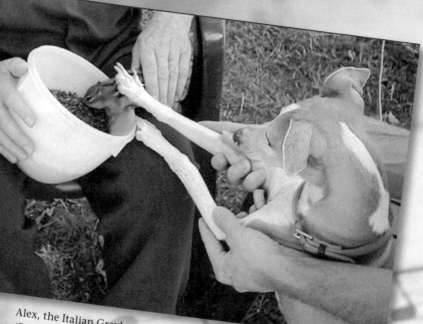

Alex, the Italian Greyhound, strokes Junko, the Chipmunk.
(Partially visible: Junko Ichikawa and Bill Finizio.)

Seymour feeds Junko, the Chipmunk.

INTERMEZZO:
Creativity, Solitude, and Self-Love

Andrew: I would now like to talk about some qualities that I have observed in you which are often seen in spiritual seekers. My hope is discussing these qualities will help our readers consider how they might nurture similar qualities in themselves. The first is that you are genuinely far more interested in exploring the person in front of you than you are in having the attention on yourself. You have a temperament which turns the whole of you towards the other. Everybody feels in your presence that they're seen and they're loved.

Seymour: Yes. Even right now when I'm talking with you, I feel I don't exist. The only person that exists is you. I'm completely involved in you.

Andrew: It's the same thing when you're giving a master class. I've seen you so many times sit quietly, and there's a moment when I can see that you almost completely vanish and become the young man or young woman play-ing. That's what gives you your extraordinary sensitivity to who they are and what they need.

Seymour: I do that with every person I'm with. I become that person. And I think it touches them because they know that I have their well-being, their feelings, their sensitivities at heart.

Andrew: Yes, and I think it actually enchants people. In our culture hardly anyone is paying any attention to anyone else. Hardly anyone knows the color of your eyes because they're so self-absorbed. So to be in the presence of somebody who truly listens to you and loves you, and pays attention to you, is intoxicating. And this is one of the great sources of your charm for all the people who love you.

Seymour: I'm so grateful that you see that about me.

Andrew: I think I sometimes do the same thing. I have a natural gift for vanishing into the person in front of me.

Seymour: I agree. It's a gift that the finest teachers have. They become their pupils. They take on all their aspects for one purpose only—to help them.

Andrew: I think it goes even deeper than that. I think the best teachers are motivated by a very broad love. And love dictates that emptying of the self to receive the other. That's what love is. When you're in the presence of a great friend or even a beloved animal, your whole being is poured out in adoration, your whole being becomes like an invisible receiver of that beloved being.

Seymour: I agree with you. When I'm with people, I'm aware of their suffering. In contrast to the person that I'm with, I feel that I've been blessed, and that I have an enormous sense of compassion. Therefore, I only want to help them.

Andrew: And that brings us to another very important quality that you have. You are bathed in serenity. You have been blessed. You haven't been just lucky. You haven't just had certain privileges. You haven't simply been fortunate enough to have a good mother, and some wonderful teachers. Something even greater has happened to you; your deepest spirit has been bathed in serenity and peace and joy.

Seymour: I think it's true. And I'm very grateful for that. So, when I'm with someone else, I want to help them to feel the same as I do.

Andrew: People come to you for the emanation of joy that you give them. The healing joy that comes from you naturally. But at the same time it is the depth of this inner blessing that also separates you secretly from others. That joy comes from the most secret part of you, which they may never know. That blessing, that hidden side.

Seymour: You mean they may never be the recipient of it themselves?

Andrew: Right.

Seymour: And does this frustrate them?

Andrew: I don't think so. As long as they know where to go to bathe in the well.

Seymour: Where do you think this blessing comes from?

Andrew: The source of this rare kind of blessing is what I would call divine grace. But let us turn to another quality that we share and that is a very deep love of solitude. People who love solitude are always somewhat mysterious because you know that they experience in solitude a depth of relationship that they may not experience even with their closest friends or with their lovers.

Seymour: You pinpointed something that is absolutely true. Much as I love to be with certain people, I would prefer to be by myself. I'm not sure why it is that I prefer to be alone, but my immediate response is that when I'm alone, I have certain desires and impulses that I have to pay attention to, especially creative stirrings that have to give birth to something. They can't find fruition when I'm with someone else. I often find people a disturbance and a distraction to something within me that wants to come out and express itself. That's the basic reason why I need to be alone. I need to have intimacy with that secret world inside of me. It demands my attention. I can't turn my back on it.

Andrew: From observing you, I think that there are a number of important reasons why you love to be alone. The first is that you are an exceptionally sensitive person and you've kept this very profound, rich, deep sensitivity alive in your mind, in your heart, and in your body. So constantly coming into connection with people who are suffering and jangled and broken is an enormous demand on your energy. The more sensitive you are, the more difficult it is to constantly be around people because so much pain, rage, dislocation, neurosis is coming from them, and you're very, very alert to all of those things. That's the first reason. Is that accurate?

Seymour: Yes. Well, when I'm with people who are in need, I want to help them, and this drains me.

Andrew: That's the second reason. I've observed that you're incapable of not reaching out to another person, another being. Your whole being instinctually reaches out to help, serve, and give whatever you can, and that exhausts you over time. That's one of the reasons why you've learned over your whole life to protect yourself from people, because you cannot resist and don't want to resist the impulse inside your heart to give whatever you have that could help.

Seymour: You just called up something else that I have inadvertently kept hidden until this moment. I'm about to say it. Oh, Andrew, this is not very nice. But I'm going to say it anyway.

Andrew: What is it?

Seymour: Far too often, when I'm with someone too long, they begin to reveal certain characteristics that repel me. So part of the reason why I prefer to be alone is because I want to protect myself from being disillusioned.

Andrew: I think it's very wise. I think that part of the reason why we all need to be alone is to be in connection with what cannot disillusion. This is how I see it.

Seymour: Exactly, I can't be disillusioned when I'm alone, because I'm in tune with the secret world that whispers things to me. They're never disappointing. It's my creative world pouring out of my *spiritual reservoir.*

Andrew: Well, that's the third reason. I don't think that anyone who has committed himself or herself to the work of art as deeply as you and I have can afford to ignore the need for solitude and seclusion, because deepest creative rhythms only start to percolate in solitude.

Seymour: Oh, of course. If anyone was here and I tried to sit at the piano and compose, I wouldn't be able to do it. I would be concerned about their needs, or what they're thinking. They would end up being a distraction to me.

Andrew: You once told me a wonderful story about a student coming to take a lesson from the great Wanda Landowska. The student was ushered into the waiting room and told to wait as Madame Landowska was in the garden, "communing with Bach."

Seymour: Yes, it's a wonderful story. And it's also completely real.

Andrew: I have no doubt of that. And in fact one of the reasons why I love seclusion and solitude is that I can commune with Rumi. I can commune with Shakespeare. I can commune with Montaigne and Rilke. We've talked a lot about friendship, but why would we confine friendship just to the people we meet in the body? What about the souls we meet in books and in music? When you come to Maine, in this garden, you do commune with Bach. You commune with Mozart. You commune with Brahms.

Seymour: Oh, I certainly do. Schubert is my best friend. He whispers secrets in my ear while I play his music.

Andrew: That's why you love the seclusion, for that friendship to flower completely.

Seymour: Of course. You and I share a lot.

Andrew: It's very hard to describe to people who haven't experienced it, what it's like to be in solitude with someone you love with your whole being, someone who matters to you as much as life itself, but someone who is no longer in their body.

Seymour: Yes, and sometimes people think you are crazy or they resent that kind of mystical "conversation" because it means a rejection of them.

Andrew: So my love of Rumi makes someone feel upset because they can't compete with Rumi? But why would they ever want to compete with Rumi? Who could compete with Rumi?

Seymour: Well, it's their ego. They're thinking, *So, you'd rather be with a dead person than with me?*

Andrew: But Schubert isn't dead for you. Schubert is more alive than anyone for you.

Seymour: But of course.

Andrew: Rumi is more alive than anyone for me.

Seymour: But most people don't know that. They've never experienced that.

Andrew: So one of the reasons why we love seclusion is that it allows us to protect these sacred friendships that so many people don't understand.

Seymour: I think so.

Andrew: And it seems to me that people like us who have opened our sensibilities to connections in the spirit world have a huge variety of relationships at a very deep level which many people don't. And the fact that some of these relationships are with beings that are so-called dead, with great musicians, poets, artists, etc., why wouldn't that be a wonderful invitation to others to seek out those relationships as well?

I just spent the most amazing day in Paris with fifty of Velázquez's paintings. To me Velázquez is the greatest painter who ever lived, greater than Rembrandt, Vermeer, and I never understood why I love him so, it's a mystery to me.

Seymour: Well, there again, you don't have to explain it.

Andrew: No, I don't.

Seymour: You just experience it.

Andrew: I accept it. But when I heard that there was going to be an exhibition of fifty of his paintings in Paris, I didn't tell anybody, any of my Parisian friends, because they would have insisted on coming with me. I went in the early morning to be the first person there, and I spent the whole day with Velázquez. I went alone to be with him.

Seymour: How wonderful.

Andrew: I wanted to be with this great, lucid, terrible, stark, unbelievably precise genius who for me expresses the mystery of human suffering and human nobility more intensely than any other painter.

Seymour: How fascinating.

Andrew: And anybody else's presence there would have been a screen between the friendship of my soul with his.

Seymour: Of course. But it would take a profoundly sensitive person, and someone who had their own passions.

Andrew: Their own love of him.

Seymour: To understand your need to be alone.

Andrew: Being alone is quite terrifying to some people. Many people think finding the right relationship or friendship is the most important thing—finding someone to love. But ultimately the most important person to love may be yourself. I remember seeing a film about relationships and realizing yourself. The most moving moment in the film is when you see a man in his forties who is living alone, the person who makes the film asks him why he's so happy. And he says, "At last, I have fallen in love with myself, and I have come to meet myself, and I feel that this is the true meaning of life." He doesn't say, "I won't have a relationship." He's saying something more profound, he's saying that the real relationship we are on the earth to have is with the depths and powers and energies and radiances of our own deepest self.

Seymour: Andrew, I wholeheartedly identify with that. That's why I always have said that one of the chief goals in life is to learn to love yourself.

Andrew: Rilke says in *Letters to a Young Poet* that love, authentic love, is two solitudes that border, protect, and salute each other.

Seymour: Beautiful.

Andrew: Border: do not encroach on each other; protect: because they realize how important the other's solitude is to the depths of themselves; and salute: because they understand the pain, the rigor, and the nobility of solitude.

Seymour: Because they've gone through it themselves, of course.

Andrew: Yes. To me that is the ultimate statement about love, as I understand it at this moment in my life.

Seymour: Another wonderful definition of true love is "I want only what's good for my lover, even at the expense of my own needs." I also read a most illuminating definition of love as being "a compassionate understanding of another person's faults."

Andrew: I hear you.

Seymour: Do you feel the same?

Andrew: I feel that this is the happiest period of my life, because I expect very much less from relationships now than I ever did. I put my deepest trust in my relationship with the beloved, and I put my deepest energy in my relationship with my own spiritual practice and dedication to helping others. And I've found that that has, over time, made me much less demanding in my friendships and in my love affairs and much less expectant of redemption through them, which is always, I think, a fantasy and a mistake.

Seymour: I'm not ashamed to say that I enjoy loving myself, and I know how important that is because if you don't love yourself, you won't be able to love anyone else.

Andrew: What do you actually mean by "loving yourself"? I ask because we live in such a narcissistic culture where people are endlessly talking about loving themselves and it seems to me to be just pampering oneself and going on and on about one's own crises and traumas and needs. And that to me is not loving oneself; it is just being obsessed with oneself. What is the difference between being truly loving of oneself and being obsessed with oneself?

Seymour: No one ever asked me that question before. But now that you raised this issue, something came to mind: we have to express ourselves honestly, and to say what we really feel. When I say that I love myself, it's because I have accepted certain challenges in my life and brought them to fruition, some more successfully than others. If I'm composing a piece, I start to improvise and I write down a motif that appeals to me. And now I sit in stillness listening in my mind's ear for the inevitable continuation of the motif I wrote down. It can't be superficial; it has to stem from what I've already done. I make an attempt, but it's false. The next attempt is far worse. Hold on, I'm getting closer. And now I find what has to emanate from the last tone of the motif. When I do that, it's like having my own loving arms around me, and I say to myself, *You're such a good person, I love you for that.* We can also use the word *proud.* "I'm proud of myself." But the word *love* springs from one's *spiritual reservoir.*

Andrew: In Tibetan Buddhism and in Sufism, there is a wonderful phrase called "divine pride," and it's considered a sign of real awakening to have divine pride, to really acknowledge the depth and richness of the qualities of generosity, courage, and passion that live in you. The difference between having divine pride and being narcissistic is that when you're narcissistic, you claim those qualities for yourself. But when you are *awake* you are aware that those qualities are within you and you dedicate them to life, to others, to creativity.

Seymour: How beautiful. In other words, what I have experienced becomes a means of sharing revelations with everyone else.

Andrew: Yes.

Seymour: I wanted to add that when I feel a self-love, or a pride in my accomplishments, I'm fully aware that it didn't come from me. So, as I mentioned earlier, I imagine a place within me that I call a *spiritual reservoir.* It's in all living things, animals as well. It connects us all. I'm aware that when I find a musical solution during composing that I've tapped the *spiritual reservoir* for the answer, inside of me, and not outside.

Andrew: And it belongs to everything and everyone.

Seymour: I like the idea of "divine" pride because it's clearly not personal or egotistic. So it's a blessing.

Andrew: For me, what you call a *spiritual reservoir* is like a great ocean of light, and I feel myself a drop of that ocean. So whatever arises in me, whatever I can give comes through me but is the ocean's to give.

Seymour: So you become lesser.

Andrew: My goal is to disappear into the depth of what has been given to me to give.

Seymour: I feel the same.

Andrew: You just mentioned that the *spiritual reservoir* is in all things—connecting us to all, including our beloved animals. Everything seems to dissolve when we surrender to the simple unconditional love we can experience when we are in the presence of our beloved animal friends. That's where all differences melt and we can simply give and receive love on a level that is wordless and profound.

Seymour: Yes, you and I, Andrew, come closest to each other in our shared love of animals, in our delight at their capacity for unconditional love and playfulness and mystery. I realized this when you rang me last February and told me that your beloved golden tabby, Topaz, had died at the tragically early age of five. You were as devastated as if you were a parent who had lost a child, and you spoke about him as someone who had taught you the truth of life.

Andrew: I was inconsolable for months.

Seymour: Believe me, I understand. Animals have always been a part of my life since I was born. My parents, too, adored pets. Whatever would have happened to me if I was born to parents who hated animals?

My mother told me that I was born in the Saint Barnabas Hospital in Newark, New Jersey. When she took me home from the hospital and placed me in a crib, Margie, our Boston bulldog leapt into the crib, snuggled next to me, and simply adopted me.

I too had a cat I adored, and was adored by and whose death devastated me. His name was Köchel. Köchel was one of the most adorable characters that you could meet. He sat to the left on my piano music desk while I practiced and taught. Whenever I or my pupils turned a page, he reached out with his paw to smooth it down. You can just imagine how delighted my pupils were at his antics. When I left the piano, he jumped onto my bench as though he were now the music teacher. Whenever I would try out programs in my studio, Köchel sat in the middle of the room and waited patiently for me to launch into a slow movement whereupon Köchel would "join in" with various "cat" sounds—sometimes soft little sounds and sometimes loud and protesting yowls. He must have thought that he could then be heard over softer playing. One evening, when I began the second movement of Beethoven's Sonata op. 111, Köchel emitted the loudest roar in his guttural repertoire. That movement is certainly not conducive to humor. But when Köchel did that, the entire room broke up, me included.

We adored each other. Köchel was only happy when he was pressed against me. Naturally he slept in the crook of my left arm and purred through the night. In fact I never heard a cat purr as often as Köchel did. His purring mechanism seemed never to get out of oil!

When Köchel was seventeen, he developed cancer of his jaw and couldn't eat any longer. That didn't diminish the love he lavished upon me. He even continued to purr as he was being put to rest. His sister, Sheila, followed him a year later.

I was so grief-stricken at his passing that I unplugged the phone in my apartment for three days. I created a piano book for children in his memory.

Andrew: That is so moving. Now tell me about this menagerie of animal friends you have here in Maine.

Seymour: Well, Andrew, I began spending my summers in Maine in 1968. My two cats always rode up with me. They adored the country and the fresh air. I had never seen a raccoon until I moved to Maine. So one night, I left a piece of Betty Crocker cake on a table outside my studio. It didn't take long for a raccoon to appear. She devoured the cake, climbed the five steps to my studio door, and looked at me and my two cats with the most pleading expression.

It didn't take long for us to establish a sweet friendship. She allowed me to sit outside with her, and she would often stroke my hand with the velvety part of her paw. I simply melted when she did that. Betty learned to take marshmallows from my mouth without ever touching me.

Andrew: Raccoons are not known to be people-friendly so that is quite a story. Now tell me about the other critters you have bewitched.

Seymour: For starters my adorable chipmunks. One chipmunk whom I called Belinda returned for nine successive summers.

More recently, another darling came into my life. I named her Junko, after one of my favorite pupils.

And finally, there was Bill, the most friendly red squirrel I have ever encountered.

And now let me tell you about a remarkable event that happened. One day I was visited by my close friend Bill, who had an adorable greyhound named Alex. Junko was in my hand nearby enjoying sunflower seeds. Bill brought Alex over and very carefully picked up one of Alex's paws and stroked tiny little Junko's face. Junko went right on eating as though this was a normal experience for her, and Alex must have thought that this is merely an extension of his mission—to extend love to all living things.

I don't know how you feel when animals become our friends, but I feel blessed. I say to myself, *In the presence of a chipmunk, I'm a giant.* You know, they start out by being terrified of you when they see you. That they would end up coming into my studio, sit on my lap, and allow me to pet them, is for me the greatest form of trust. I feel so honored that they allow me to come into their lives. And then, I whisper to myself, *You must be a good person for them to love you like that.*

Andrew: Well you know, I've spent a great many years studying the lives of some of the great saints and prophets of humanity, and one of the things I've noticed is that in nearly every case he or she has been very close to animals. For example, last time I was in Konya visiting Rumi's tomb, I was standing next to an old lady who spoke broken English, and we became friends. She said, "You know who's in the tomb with him?"

And I said, "There's nobody in that tomb with Rumi; this is the most famous tomb in Islam apart from the tomb of the prophet."

And she came back with "Oh no, you're wrong."

Rumi, she told me, had a favorite cat at the end of his life. And when he was dying, the cat jumped off the bed the moment he left the earth, and went and hid in the house, and starved herself to death. So when it came time for Rumi to be buried, Rumi was buried with the cat on his heart. And this was absolutely unprecedented in Islam. A great saint is never buried with anything, but Rumi's daughter insisted that the cat that Rumi loved was placed on his heart center. And when she was asked why, she said, "Because my father was a friend to all creation."

In one of his letters, Rumi wrote something I cherish deeply: "Adore and love the Beloved with your whole being and He will reveal to you that each thing in the universe is a vessel full to the brim with wisdom and beauty. Each thing He will show you is one drop from the boundless river of His infinite beauty." Perhaps the greatest joy of both of our lives, Seymour, is that we both, through our love of animals, have come to know what those glorious words mean.

Seymour: You know what happened one year about ten years ago? I went outside to sit by the sea, when a chickadee landed on my shoulder.

Andrew: A wild chickadee landed on your shoulder?

Seymour: That's right. So I moved my left finger over to my shoulder and it stepped onto my finger. I held it in front of me and it looked into my eyes. I had a container of sunflower seeds nearby and put some sunflower seeds in my right palm. The chickadee hopped into my palm, took a sunflower seed in its beak and flew away. And then it came right back. So, while it was resting on my finger, I walked into my studio. That was the wrong thing to do. It flew onto a windowsill and tried to get out. It mistook the window for freedom, and it panicked. It flew around throwing itself at the windows. I went over to it and put my finger under its claws. This calmed it immediately. It came again onto my finger and I led it to the open door of my studio. It flew away, and I never saw it again. But I was so amazed to be in touch with the wild bird kingdom. I felt it was a blessing.

Andrew: An old Native American shaman once told me that his tribe believed that when you die, you go to a bridge, and that bridge has on it all the animals that you have encountered in your life. And it's they who choose whether you can cross over the bridge to a new life, so he said, "How you treat the animals in your life shows what kind of a person you really are."

Seymour: Oh how interesting.

Andrew: So I feel that when you come to that moment when you do leave the earth, you'll be before that bridge and on it will be your childhood dog, and your Siamese cats, and the parrots and all the chipmunks that you've loved and who have loved you, and they will let you cross over. You can be assured of that.

Seymour: Will my pets come with me?

Andrew: If there is a heaven without animals, I have no desire to go there.

Seymour: But seriously, Andrew, you know I don't believe in heaven or hell or the afterlife. But I do think it's possible to achieve moments of heaven here on earth. What is needed is to become attuned to one's *spiritual reservoir*, to nourish oneself in solitude, to develop the ability to experience self-love, to be open to the gifts of soul friends and animals, and finally to plumb the depths of one's desire and passion in an artistic way allowing that artistic expression to influence how we live.

PART IV

TEACHING

1.

The Mysteries of Giving and Receiving

Andrew: I think one of the deepest reasons that people are so drawn to you is because you are the archetype of the inspired, humble, loving teacher. Let's talk about teaching.

Seymour: Before I discuss teaching, I need to address something that gets brought up frequently, namely, my having given up performing. I never gave up my ability to be a concert pianist. That has been evolving all the time, even after I quit my solo career. My desire to search for the truth of what a specific note, say a B-flat or a G-sharp, means in a particular musical phrase has never stopped. And revelation upon revelation has appeared to me. So that part of me has continued in my practicing. I also continued to play chamber music with the greatest players and in the world's finest venues.

And that feeds into my teaching. I don't believe that I would be a good teacher if I ever stopped playing. When we were discussing music the other day, I told you that the deepest sensitivity that a musician has for shaping a phrase is inborn. It can't be taught. Nevertheless, a good teacher can help pupils simulate such shaping. Similarly, I believe that the qualities that make for good teaching are inborn. At the same time, pedagogical techniques can be passed on to pupils from one generation to another, thus perpetuating the tradition of the finest teaching.

And speaking of teaching, I would like to say that as soon as you emerge from the guest bedroom and start to talk to me, you're teaching me all the time.

Andrew: Really?

Seymour: Yes, really. It's part of your nature. I learn things from you all the time. I listen to how you form sentences. But mostly, I'm struck by the passion that is behind every phrase that you speak. It comes from a very deep center within you, perhaps from your *spiritual reservoir?*

Andrew: Thank you. I love teaching! So tell me how it all started for you.

Seymour: When I was fifteen, I studied with the most wonderful teacher, my first real teacher, in Newark, New Jersey. Her name was Clara Husserl. Her husband was the cousin of the famous philosopher Edmund Husserl. If you mention the name Husserl to a philosophy major, they are awestruck.

Andrew: He's one of the great founders of modern linguistics.

Seymour: So you know the name?

Andrew: Yes.

Seymour: Clara Husserl had four children, and each one excelled in a particular field: Franz was a famous psychiatrist. Paul had a wide and varied career: he was a feature writer and reporter for *Time* and *Cinema Arts* magazines and later became managing editor of *The March of Time*. During World War II, he served overseas as combat photographer under General Douglas MacArthur. After the war, he became night news editor of NBC in New York and film coordinator for the original *Today* show; Adelaide was an actress and had a TV show for children. Clara Husserl's eldest child was pianist Hortense Monath. She was the first woman to play with Toscanini and the founder of a famous music series entitled New Friends of Music. She was a formidable pianist and a favorite pupil of Artur Schnabel. I knew her very well. She was the typical prima donna type, and was totally spoiled by having married twice to very rich and prominent men. So now you can picture the environment in which I found myself when I studied with Clara Husserl. I felt like a member of her family, so I addressed her as Aunt Clara.

Andrew: How ever did you meet this wonderful woman?

Seymour: Andrew, you won't believe how I met her. Remember how my mother in her innocence found my first teacher by asking the milkman? Well this time, my mother visited a friend in the hospital and happened to mention that I loved to play the piano. Her friend told her that the finest teacher in Newark was Clara Husserl. So that's how I met her. We adored each other from the first meeting. She undertook the responsibility for my total development. For one thing, she supplied me with reading matter that would have challenged a Ph.D. candidate. How I at fifteen, having read only the books assigned to me in school, ever digested works by Nietzsche and Goethe, for example, astonishes me to this day. I would have been lost entirely had it not been for Aunt Clara's own comments, which filled the margins of practically every page. Taking the form of rebuttals and affirmations, they led me to understand, in part at least, the complicated subjects under discussion. Occasionally, some aspect of the text would inspire Aunt Clara to compose a poem, which she would then scribble in a burst of inspiration onto the front or back pages of the book. To be sure, I was unsophisticated and given to extremes of sentimentality myself. Yet, even I winced at the awkward rhymes, the meter, and the naive content of those poems. And more than once, I felt compelled to utter out loud, "Oh, no . . ."

Andrew: Did Madame Husserl take you out on the town with her or to concerts?

Seymour: Aunt Clara and I went everywhere together. It was she, for instance, who took me to Carnegie Hall for the first time to hear the famed Artur Schnabel. He was at that time one of the first pianists to perform Beethoven's thirty-two sonatas in public. He was also a famous teacher. As a matter of fact, Sir Clifford Curzon, the greatest teacher I ever studied with, was his pupil. Hortense and Madame Schnabel, a well-known singer of lieder, sat in a box to our right. Schnabel's performance of the *Waldstein* Sonata, as well as his imposing presence at the keyboard, has remained indelibly imprinted in my mind: the stillness of his body; the quiet, strong hands; and the extraordinary range of dynamics emanating from the piano—all reminded me of Aunt Clara's playing. As a matter of fact, Schnabel was himself a pupil of Leschetizky, the famed Viennese pedagogue. And I remember thinking how fortunate I was to be in such good hands.

Andrew: Seymour, she sounds wonderful and so generous. Was she a happy woman?

Seymour: Having the best pupils in New Jersey, and basking in the glow of her own children's successes, Aunt Clara ought to have enjoyed her life to the fullest. Yet she clearly missed the intellectual climate of Vienna that she had experienced during her student days. At every opportunity, therefore, she tried to re-create that climate as best as she could. Vivid in her memory were the beer halls and the stimulating discussions held there among the Leschetizky pupils. She no doubt thought that her Sonny was deprived of something vital to his personal growth: Nietzsche, Goethe, and beer halls, too, would evidently improve my playing. Thus one evening, upon returning to Newark from one of our forays into New York City, Aunt Clara took me to a local bar around the corner from her home. To call it seedy would be a generous assessment of its appearance. Dirty and disheveled, it looked like a hangout for Newark's lowlife. But all bars have beer on tap, and this was what interested Aunt Clara. I can scarcely imagine what the bartender and all of those derelicts must have thought at the sight of an elderly, aristocratic-looking woman and a teenage boy sitting at a table guzzling beer. That I at fifteen was served at all was astonishing in itself. Aunt Clara, completely oblivious to the eyes upon us, calmly sipped her beer and proceeded to discuss the concert that we had attended that evening. After an hour or so, feeling quite satisfied that she had given her Sonny a sampling of Bohemian life, she decided to call it a night. She arose from her seat, went directly up to the bartender to pay him, and walked out with nonchalant dignity. I followed her, with a somewhat lighter step than that with which I had entered the bar.

Aunt Clara may have had her eccentric ways, but she was the paragon of piano playing. Whatever she assigned me, I learned. And if her ambitions for me far exceeded my capabilities, I was not aware of this in the slightest: concerti by Mozart, Beethoven, Tchaikovsky, Schumann, and Liszt; all the difficult Beethoven sonatas; virtuoso works by Chopin and Liszt; and Schubert's *Wanderer* Fantasy, which she asked me to learn in one week for her yearly student recital—all of this, and more, I practiced and performed simply because she suggested it.

Andrew: And what did Clara Husserl teach you?

Seymour: While I adored Aunt Clara and was enthralled by her playing, I can't say that she instructed me technically or musically. I was keen enough, nevertheless, to listen to her phrasing and observe her physical movements at the piano. But above everything else, I was inspired to be in her presence. She told me that when she was seventeen, she studied with Leschetizky in Vienna. He was one of the most famous pedagogues that ever lived. She told me that the Professor told her she had *goldene Hände*, "golden hands." Whenever she played examples for me during lessons, everything seemed to flow naturally

from her hands. Yet, I don't think she knew why her playing sounded so beautiful. She thought that she and I were
similar in that we were natural pianists. So we just com-
muned with each other.

She tried to create contacts for me, because she thought
I was going to have a major career. For example, she knew
John Ortiz who was head of the Baldwin piano company.
The Baldwin company had fortunes of money. So they just
gave pianos to anyone who was going to be a so-called
Baldwin Artist, and Leonard Bernstein was one of them.
Mrs. Husserl contacted Mr. Ortiz and arranged for me to
audition for him. I was sixteen, and my reason told me that
I was certainly not ready to have a big career. Yet suddenly
I found myself in Mr. Ortiz's office and sitting before a gorgeous Baldwin concert grand. Andrew, I don't know what
possessed me, but to this day I don't think I could play
better than I did on that occasion. I just knocked them
out. First I played the Chopin Polonaise in F-sharp Minor,
and then one of the most difficult virtuoso pieces of Liszt
called *Gnomenreigen*, "Dance of the Gnomes." Everything
seemed to roll out of my fingers, as though someone else
was doing the playing.

When I finished the Liszt, Mr. Ortiz didn't say a word.
He went to the telephone and called Leonard Bernstein.
The message on the answering machine stated that Lenny
had gone to the hospital to have an appendectomy. So
Mr. Ortiz left him the following message: "Dear Lenny,
this is John Ortiz. I just heard the most gifted pianist I've
ever heard. His name is Seymour Bernstein. Bernstein and
Bernstein have to get together." I never heard anything
more about it. That was it. Frankly speaking, I was relieved
because I really wasn't ready for the big time.

As I said earlier, Aunt Clara had the best pupils in all
of New Jersey, but she thought that they didn't practice

properly. So when I was fifteen she arranged for me to go to their homes and supervise their practicing. As I think about it now, I wonder why she had so much faith in me so as to trust me with her pupils. After all, I never taught anyone before. She did, however, believe that she and I were natural pianists, and I suppose she knew that I would steer her pupils in the right direction. After each day in high school, I went to Aunt Clara's pupils' homes. It was not only the beginning of my teaching career, but it was also the first time I earned money through music. I remember having instinctive responses to everything I heard and saw the pupil do. By the end of the year, I earned enough money to pay off my first Steinway grand, a model L (5' 10½") that I bought from Steinway & Sons in New York City. The following year I started to get private pupils. I adored working through difficult passages with pupils and helping them solve problems right then and there. I realized even then what a privilege it was to make a contribution to others.

Andrew: So teaching for you is a way of helping the person in front of you develop the skills and the discipline and the intuition with which they can enter music and represent music and so be blessed by music. In teaching, you help them discover themselves as skillful interpreters of this great art. And so they learn to feel deeply good about themselves.

Seymour: I wish that I would have been able to say it exactly as you did. You said it perfectly. Yes, that's exactly what it is. Look here: my pupils and I are serving our art. I'm helping them, and together we're preserving the sacred art of music.

Andrew: How do you advise a pupil about how to study a new piece? Knowing you, Seymour, you have a plan that can help.

Seymour: I do have a plan. I've narrowed it down to four stages of learning: spontaneity, awareness, commitment, and synthesis. About the first stage, *spontaneity*, who has not felt the impact of love at first sight? In music, it may awaken to a theme, a subtle harmonic modulation, or an inner harmonic voice. In this first stage, feelings are all spontaneous and charged with currents of passionate longing. Thought and reason are replaced with exultation. Since I only learn pieces that I love, the first stage of sight-reading the piece is a love at first sight experience. As I play a phrase without preconceived musical or technical ideas, the music itself tells me what it wants to do. This presupposes that you are a good sight reader. Sight-reading ought to be a major priority in teaching. Without that ability, the wonders of music are closed to you.

Andrew: Say more about what happens to you in the first stage.

Seymour: When I am most receptive, I have the feeling that I am not playing at all, but rather *being* played. In short, the music plays me, not only through my emotional and intellectual worlds, but also through my entire body. When the sound that emerges from the piano corresponds to my musical concept, I experience a sense of triumph. I feel empowered to conquer other challenges, both musical and personal. I also feel worthy to help others shed their sense of victimization and meet challenges head on.

Andrew: How do you keep this first magical response alive?

Seymour: To retain this initial spontaneity over the long course of studying a piece, or knowing a person, is a difficult task. The problem is that spontaneity left unattended too long disintegrates rapidly through its own uncontrolled force. Like blind infatuation, it engenders feelings that tend to fluctuate and, in some cases, vanish altogether.

Paradoxically, spontaneity can only be tempered through discipline. This is because heady and rapturous first love often tends to grow less dependable the more easily it is gratified. Boredom then replaces ardor, and all is lost in disenchantment. Such disenchantment is caused by a lack of discipline, or an unwillingness to sacrifice one's freedom to the requirements of one's love.

At this point, stage two begins—*awareness*. There are two ways to maintain spontaneity: one is through observation, the other, through analysis. Together, observation and analysis lead you to *awareness* that illuminates your love and encourages it to endure.

Andrew: So this awareness stage is one where deep feeling becomes honed and tempered by thought.

Seymour: Yes, absolutely. Some musicians don't want to face awareness and observation. Like lovers, they don't want to be awakened from a dream. They feel that analysis will place limits on their freedom of expression. But music, after all, sets limits on how we express ourselves. All notational markings, for example, have to be honored with our deepest concentration. Curiously, the analysis of such musical details is what ultimately feeds spontaneity.

In short, it is necessary to take music, or a person, into your mind, as well as your heart.

We have to consider two points: first, if observation and analysis adversely affect your spontaneity, then your initial love was no doubt mere infatuation. Second, it is actually possible to analyze a genuine love out of existence. To prevent this, you must suspend analysis from time to time and play through the entire composition, reliving your first encounter with it. Each time you repeat this experience, your control over feeling and thinking enlarges, until your original response to music is rekindled and even intensified.

There are times when trying to fathom what a composer meant is like pondering the meaning of a friend's behavior. The more we search for answers, the less confident we feel. At moments like this, even the most ardent student is tempted to abandon his work on one composition and look for refuge in another: "I wasn't meant to play Beethoven. I ought to stick with Mozart. He's less ponderous," etc. But the moment you turn from one half-completed task to another, you set a dangerous precedent for yourself. Chances are you will justify a second abandonment and even a third until you become a person who just wants to enjoy momentary pleasures.

Andrew: How do you prevent this?

Seymour: The only thing that can prevent this is *commitment* to a genuine purpose. This is stage three. If for example you are humbled by the genius of a Beethoven, Schubert, or Chopin, you must grow large enough in spirit and accomplishment to meet them on their own terms. "I love that piece, and I am going to master it even if it takes the rest of my life." From that moment on, the piece is yours because you have earned it. And your relationship with a person who you spontaneously loved and then got disillusioned with turns out to be more serious than you thought. Without commitment, or perseverance, nothing of importance can ever be achieved.

Having survived these three stages, you will become enlightened when you enter the final stage—*synthesis*. At this stage, everything you felt, dreamed of, and understood intuitively in your first moment of love is realized and fulfilled, but with this difference: it is all informed with knowledge and awareness. Armed with this metaknowledge, you are now ready to gratify others with the beauty you have absorbed into yourself. You are ready to perform.

Andrew: I love your progression of the four stages—spontaneity, awareness, commitment, synthesis. They correspond uncannily with how I approach integrating my being with a new sacred practice or studying and attempting to understand a vision of a great mystical work by one of the masters, Teresa of Ávila or Ibn Arabi, or my favorite, the great Flemish mystic Ruysbroeck, whose prose is, for me, divine music almost as great and challenging as Bach's.

When you said just now "You are ready to perform," I was deeply moved because it seemed to me that you were saying that it's only when you have submitted to the beautiful rigor of such a necessarily challenging process, and arrived at the end of it, that you're truly ready to serve the great, complex, sacred art that is music.

It's an immense responsibility of the whole being, isn't it? To really execute a Beethoven sonata or a Mozart sonata with true integrity to the composer's vision. Everything has to be given to it.

Seymour: Well, it entails an integration of our spiritual, emotional, intellectual, and physical worlds. You take away any of those components and you're not serving music. Because all of those components are within music itself. The music represents the perfect integration of all of those components. So, we have to approach music the same way. We can't just feel it, we have also to use our brains to understand each and every notational indication. And that's certainly not enough, because if we don't make a physical connection to what we're feeling and thinking, the piano won't reproduce our musical concept. Imagine synthesizing all of those components—our spiritual, emotional, intellectual, and physical worlds. Do you realize what a powerful thing that is?

Andrew, what follows is very, very important. Do you know what far too many musicians do? They achieve this synthesis musically, and they walk away from the piano and leave it there. Small wonder that many become wrecks of human beings. They fail to direct that synthesis into their everyday lives. It is a synthesis that can harmonize them.

Andrew: They don't realize, in fact, that being an interpreter of music is an invitation to personal and spiritual work of subtle harmonization that music itself is the highest example of.

Seymour: They have to learn to be interpreters of life, not just interpreters of music. All musicians should learn that lesson from working at their art. Now, the synthesis of taking what you learn through the process of practicing and performing and directing it into your everyday life can happen automatically. It happened to me automatically. But for most musicians, it has to be done consciously.

Andrew: How did it happen to you; how did you notice it?

Seymour: When I was fifteen, I observed that whenever I practiced well, and accomplished something, I felt good about myself when I left the piano. At moments like that everything else in my life seemed influenced by what went on in my practicing, especially the way I related to people. But when my practicing didn't go well, I felt out of sorts, guilty, and irritable with people. I concluded that there had to be a correlation between my practicing and life itself. I pondered whether life was influencing the way I make music, or is it the other way around—was my practicing influencing my life? Then I started to think about this: certainly life influences everything we do. Yet life is unpredictable. You can never trust what people are going to say or do. On the other hand, everything positive results when I practice conscientiously. Unlike life, there is a feeling of predictability. For after all, when Beethoven writes a B-flat, it's there for eternity. I therefore concluded that music and my practicing influences my life far more deeply than the other way around.

Andrew: You say that, and I hear you, but how you play the B-flat is everything. You have to understand why the composer needed just that note in that passage and then play it with a precisely appropriate fidelity to the composer's "sound field."

Seymour: Well, that's where our spiritual, emotional, intellectual, and physical attitudes come in.

Andrew: That's where the knowledge and absorption of the whole tradition comes in, the whole way of being with the music that comes down through the great pianists, through the great composers.

Seymour: I'm not a great musician; I'm just a very serious one. We already know who the great ones are. I can't compete with them. I don't have any qualms about being lesser than they are. I just want to develop as much as I can with whatever gifts I have. But I have to tell you that I consider myself blessed because when I sight-read music and confront it for the first time, it's analogous to love at first sight when you meet certain people. You don't know anything about that person, but something triggers that love. There are certain pieces that I instantly fall in love with. As I play them, my vocal chords get activated. It's as though I'm exhaling the music through singing. Somehow the music takes hold of me. I have the feeling that there is a special body part inside of me. And this body part gets permeated with the music and *plays me*. It's telling me what to do. It's analogous to someone whispering secrets in your ear: "Now go softer, now go louder, now move ahead, now take a little time." In short I have the feeling that I am *being played*. It's one of the most satisfying, beneficial, inspirational, and, at the same time, mysterious experiences that I can think of. It makes me exceedingly joyful. And when I realize what the music is telling me, I can't wait to share it with my pupils. They sense that I'm telling them something sacred that they didn't know. Imbued with this new information, my pupils are elated. The circle is completed.

2.

The Best Teacher:
Sir Clifford

Andrew: You studied with one of the greatest pianists—Clifford Curzon. Was he a great teacher?

Seymour: He was the greatest teacher I ever had. And by the way, Andrew, it's now *Sir* Clifford Curzon.

Andrew: *Sir* Clifford Curzon. It's very important that the people reading this book know of your deep love and friendship with Clifford, how he was as a teacher and how he transformed your understanding of music and encouraged you.

Seymour: I wouldn't say that he "transformed" my understanding of music. He accepted me as a pupil because I was already extremely musical. What he did was to draw out of me refinements known only to great artists such as he was. Do you know how I met him? When I was discharged from the Army, I was a wreck. I hadn't practiced properly for two years.

Andrew: After the Korean War?

Seymour: Yes. You know that I performed more as a soldier in Korea than I did in my entire lifetime. And how I ever survived that with a minimum of practicing, I don't really know. But it wasn't very good playing. I didn't have enough time to work things out. But I somehow survived. You know, I'm a survivor.

Andrew: You are.

Seymour: I always think I'm going to die, and then I always come through. Anyway, when I came out of the Army I said to myself, *If I don't challenge myself to perform at important venues, I'm not going to refine my playing.* So I did two things: I enrolled in the Fontainebleau, France, summer program where Clifford Curzon would be giving master classes; and I rented Town Hall in New York City for January 1954 to make my debut. My father paid all the expenses. But since I was very well-known in New Jersey, the hall was sold out and I actually made fifty dollars.

I always admired Clifford Curzon. He was one of my favorite artists. I'm not the only one; almost all pianists admired him, especially for his Mozart and Schubert interpretations. Now, Andrew, having come out of the Army, do you think I was ready to make my New York debut? Of course not. But if I didn't set the date, I was not going to practice eight hours a day and get my playing back at least to where it was before I was inducted into the Army. So I forced these challenges upon myself.

I went to Fontainebleau and Clifford Curzon had sent in advance a repertoire list, a syllabus of pieces he would work on. All students were to choose two pieces from that list. We were told that he would not listen to any composition that was not on that list. I chose Beethoven's *Emperor* Concerto and the Brahms Intermezzo in E Major, op. 116 no. 4, a soul cry. As it turned out, there was time for him to listen to more repertoire, so I planned to play Liszt's *Gnomenreigen*, that brilliant piece that I played for the head of the Baldwin piano company.

Now, the first day of the master class arrived. The classes took place in the palace of Fontainebleau, in a building called the *Salle du Jeu de Paume*, namely, the indoor tennis court where Napoleon played tennis. It was a huge building with the most marvelous glass windows on one side high up against the ceiling. A platform had been built at the far end to hold two concert grands. Nadia Boulanger, the faculty, and all the students were there. There was a roaring response when Clifford Curzon entered the platform. He turned to the audience and said, "I received a list of pianists that want to play for me. Only two students chose pieces from the syllabus I had sent to you. So I'm only going to listen to those students tomorrow."

Well, Andrew, the buzz of protest that ensued was rather shocking. There were serious pianists who paid a fortune in the hope of performing in those master classes. It was sheer arrogance on their part for disregarding Curzon's syllabus. And now only another girl and I would be allowed to perform for Clifford Curzon.

Andrew: And what happened in that initial meeting with him; how did he hear you?

Seymour: Oh my dear, wait until I tell you. Clifford asked if I would play the first movement of the *Emperor* Concerto for him. So I got another pianist, a student, to play the orchestra part. That day I was in the *Salle du Jeu de Paume*, practicing alone on the piano for most of the day. On the first page of the concerto, there's a trill on A-flat and B-flat. I don't think I ever trilled so brilliantly before. I believe I was inspired at the thought of playing for Clifford Curzon, whose own performance of the *Emperor* Concerto was legendary. While I was trilling, I somehow set up a vibration in the *Salle du Jeu de Paume*, and I heard a crash. The sympathetic vibrations shattered one of the windows! By the way, I returned to the *Salle du Jeu de Paume* two years later, and the window was still broken.

The day of the performance arrived. Clifford Curzon and Nadia Boulanger went to the back of the auditorium. I was sitting on the stage trying to deal with my nerves. I played the first movement to rousing applause. Frankly, I thought it was dreadful. But to my surprise, Curzon came over to me and said, "There wasn't a single dull note in the entire performance." And then he started to work with me.

I was hunched over with nerves, so the first thing he did was to stand behind me and pull me away from the piano. With my arms more extended, I began to play like I never played before. I thought, *At last: I'm getting a real piano lesson.* Of course Curzon demonstrated and played so gorgeously that I was ready to faint. We then worked on the intermezzo and *Gnomenreigen*. It was one of the great inspirations of my life.

Later that day, I met him on the street of Fontainebleau and asked him if it was possible to study with him. To my surprise he said, "Well, I'm going to take a sabbatical from performing next year. So if you could come to London, I'll teach you for six months."

Andrew: Good heavens, he offered to teach you himself for six months.

Seymour: That's right. And so, I auditioned for a Martha Baird Rockefeller grant, which paid ample money for travelling and living expenses. I asked my father for extra money because I anticipated that the lessons would cost a fortune. You see, Andrew, money was the only language that established a harmonious bond between us. I imagine that in my father's mind, he might have thought that at least he could buy my forgiveness for past transgressions. As it turned out, Curzon told me exactly what Alexander Brailowsky said when I made an attempt to pay him after my first lesson with him: "I'm sorry, but I don't teach. Therefore, I don't have a fee."

Once in London, Curzon instructed me as to what subway to take. He met me with his convertible car at the other end. It all felt as though I was in a movie. He drove me to his magnificent mansion onto which he built a veritable concert hall. It had two concert grands side by side. It was absolutely magnificent. Before I had my first lesson, I looked around and saw a plaster cast of a hand in an illuminated cabinet. I asked him whose hand it was. He sat me down on a chair, removed the hand from the cabinet, and placed it on my lap.

"Guess whose hand that is," he asked with a twinkle in his eye.

I noticed that the hand had tapered fingers and that it wasn't particularly large, and said, "Oh, that's a woman's hand."

To my utter surprise Curzon told me it was Chopin's left hand. He told me that it was the original plaster cast taken after Chopin's death, and that a very rich woman, who owned it, gave it to Curzon in admiration for his playing. You know, Andrew, I have a copy of it in New York City, but it's not the original.

Now Curzon started to work with me. I can't tell you what those lessons were like, it would be impossible.

Andrew: Try to describe one.

Seymour: Well, the first lesson was on the Brahms D-minor Concerto. It's one of the masterpieces of the romantic repertoire. Many musicians feel that Clifford Curzon's recording of it is the definitive interpretation.

Andrew: Ah.

Seymour: And the opening—

Andrew: I heard him play the D minor with Giulini, and I can still experience the thrill of his dramatic and passionate playing.

Seymour: Do you know his recording of it?

Andrew: It's magnificent.

Seymour: It's considered the best ever.

Andrew: I can see why.

Seymour: That, and certain pieces such as the *Emperor* Concerto, the Brahms D-minor Concerto, and Mozart concerti are epic performances.

Andrew: And of course Schubert, the late piano sonatas of Schubert for which he was famous. I heard him at the end of his career play the B-flat Major Sonata in the Sheldonian at Oxford. Nobody could applaud at the end because it was so sublime.

Seymour: Yes, that's how he was.

Andrew: Because the depth of the silence of the soul that he created through the music was so extraordinary.

Seymour: Yes.

Andrew: So your first lesson is with the Brahms D-minor Concerto.

Seymour: Yes. We worked on two pianos. Curzon demonstrated those sixths at the opening. They're very difficult to play legato. I was trying my best to imitate what he was doing. We never got past four measures in an hour. Curzon suddenly took his hands off of his piano and said, "You see, laddie, you traveled three thousand miles to study with me and I'm making your piano playing worse." Isn't that adorable, Andrew? The truth is, it really was getting worse because I was trying to change things and I had not yet worked out how to do what Curzon suggested effectively. In spite of my struggles, he was completely charming.

At the end of the second lesson, he told me, "For your next lesson, I would like to work on two Beethoven sonatas at the same time. I'm going to play Opus 111 in New York City next season. Have you studied it?"

I told him that coincidentally that was one piece I wanted to play for him.

"Fine. Now choose another earlier one."

I chose Op. 31, no. 2. The lesson began at 10 A.M. with that one. Hours later we came to Op. 111. The opening has the left hand alone playing forte octaves that leap a diminished seventh. I always missed that leap, so I divided the first two octaves between the hands. Namely, I played the E-flat octave with my right hand, and the F-sharp octave with my left. At the same time, I simulated the tension of what it would have sounded like when playing it with one hand alone. At least I thought I did.

Curzon said to me, "What are you doing, laddie? In making everything sound easy, you'll come crawling to the piano one day." He meant that if I continued to make difficult passages easier, I would begin to lose the discipline of meeting challenges head on and this could cause me to begin to develop a fear of the piano.

Around this time of the lesson, he suddenly said, "By the way, I have a good Nordic name, Clifford. So stop with this 'Mr. Curzon' business." I felt awkward and embarrassed addressing him by his first name. But in time I got used to it.

Back to the opening of Op. 111: "But Clifford, I always miss the second octave!"

"Well, isn't that too bad? Learn not to miss it."

So then we went on, no more discussion about that.

Now what I'm going to tell you can only be considered to be a revelation. The second movement of Op. 111, which I call "the end of the earth," is one of the most profound pieces in the history of music. You know that Op. 111 only has two movements.

Do you know Beethoven's pupil and biographer, Schindler?

Andrew: The terrible, lying Schindler.

Seymour: Yes, many things that Schindler wrote were untrue. At any rate, he asked Beethoven, "Master, aren't you going to write a third movement for Op. 111?" Beethoven must've been crushed to hear his pupil ask him such a stupid question. Realizing that Schindler didn't understand that he had come to the end of the sonata form with the final C-major chord of Op. 111, Beethoven replied, "I don't have the time."

In Thomas Mann's novel *Doctor Faustus*, he has a striking description of Op. 111. Professor Kretzschmar is giving a lecture demonstration to his pupils, and he comes to the endless trills, which he calls "chains of trills." They go on forever. Then suddenly, there's a triple trill, namely, you have to trill in three voices at the same time. Finally, the right hand continues to trill and rises into the treble, into heaven, while the left hand falls stepwise into the bass. And now when the hands are five and a half octaves apart, the trills cease and there are long tones that afford us a pause. Andrew, what can I tell you? The first time I found myself in that position, I burst into tears and thought, "I'm being crucified." Unquestionably in my mind, Beethoven graphically led us into the position of the crucifixion.

At that moment, where the hands are farthest apart, Beethoven has the word *crescendo*. It's the only time in interpreting music that I said to myself, *Sorry, baby, I'm not going to make a crescendo. I know you ask me to do it, I know who you are, you're Ludwig van Beethoven, but I cannot make a crescendo. After all I'm being crucified. I have to do exactly the opposite and make a diminuendo.*

That's what I did for Clifford Curzon. He stopped me and said, "Laddie, what are you doing?"

I said, "Clifford, don't scold me, I know there's a crescendo there, but I can't do it."

"Laddie, I understand why you can't do it, but you don't have to make a big crescendo. You need only to keep up the sound."

"No, Clifford, I can't keep up the sound. I have to die away. I can't do it."

"Why are you so stubborn, Seymour?"

I said, "Oh, Clifford, I know that I'm naughty."

Clifford responded with annoyance, "Let's go on, I don't want to discuss this anymore."

Now, Andrew, I always get gooseflesh when I come to the crux of the story. After I made my European debuts, I returned to New York City and found a package in front of my door from my friend Sheila Aldendorf. I opened it up to discover the facsimile of Beethoven's original manuscript of Op. 111. I was awestruck to see the master's original writing of this masterpiece. I couldn't resist my temptation to see what Beethoven wrote at the "crucifixion" moment in the second movement. As I turned the pages, my hands trembled as I came closer and closer to the measure in question. And then I gasped: Beethoven erased the word *crescendo* from the manuscript. I immediately phoned London and told Clifford of my discovery. He was in utter disbelief as I was. He thanked me for sharing this revelation with him.

Now Clifford came to New York City the following year to give a recital at Hunter College. He began with Op. 111. He played the opening octaves with his left hand alone and slid off of the second black-key octave as I always did before I decided to divide my hands. I said to myself, *You stubborn man. You see? You just had to adhere to Beethoven's left hand alone, and now you made scrambled eggs at your performance.* Clifford held to his principles: if Beethoven wrote those octaves to be played with the left hand alone, he was going to obey. I noticed this stubbornness throughout my studies with him. He often missed passages because he refused to rearrange them between the hands, as Horowitz, for instance, often did without having a conscience about it.

Andrew: What happened with you and Clifford was very moving because he not only became your teacher, but you also became indispensable to him. He asked you, didn't he, to really pay attention to how he was playing and help him get even better?

Seymour: That's true, Andrew. Eventually, I played a very serious role in his life. Clifford came to the United States every two years. He always performed concerti in New York City and occasionally solo recitals. I saw him every night in the basement of Steinway so long as he was in New York City. I played the orchestral parts of the concerti he was scheduled to perform, and then we would have dinner together. I always brought him fresh-squeezed orange juice, one of his favorite drinks. He could be very difficult, you know. He would suddenly fly into a rage without any cause. If, for example, my hair was uncombed due to high winds outside, he would scream, "Look at your hair! You look like a parrot!" On other occasions, I heard him speak dreadfully to his manager, and even to conductors. I have the feeling that he was schizophrenic. I also know that he suffered intensely from nervousness whenever he performed. Much as I loved his performances in public, I can tell you that I never, never heard such magisterial playing as I did when he was calm in the basement of Steinway. It was transcendent.

One evening I was completely taken aback when he stopped in the middle of Mozart's K. 488 and asked, "Now what did you think of that phrase?" Did my master really want me to criticize him? I remained still, but then he repeated, "Seriously, Seymour, what did you think of it?" I felt both embarrassed and awkward in criticizing my master, but I did discuss the phrase with him and suggested that perhaps the climax was on a different tone. And do you know, Andrew, he performed it as I suggested that same evening in Carnegie Hall. That was the beginning of the fact that my master loved to be a pupil.

On another occasion, he was to perform with Daniel Barenboim conducting. He placed me in a box in Carnegie Hall during the rehearsal, placed the full score in my lap, and gave me a pencil. "Now, write down everything that occurs to you." There was a break, and Clifford asked me to come on the stage. "Now show me all the comments you made in your score." I did, and once again he performed all of them that same night.

Once at dinner, Clifford told me that he and I had similar musical responses, and that he knew this at once when he heard me play in Fontainebleau. He then paid me the greatest compliment: "You know, laddie, I said to Lucille the other day, if I were going to choose an apprentice, you would be the only one I would consider." I could only feel an overwhelming sense of gratitude to know that my master thought so highly of me.

Andrew: What do you think he meant when he told you that he and you had similar musical responses?

Seymour: He, too, thought that he was "being played" by the music.

Andrew: I think it goes even deeper than that because what you don't know is that Clifford Curzon was my favorite pianist as a young man, and I went to see him whenever I could, from the age of about sixteen to twenty-six.

Seymour: Oh, how wonderful.

Andrew: And the reason why I did is because I heard in his playing three things that I didn't hear anywhere else. I heard a perfect seamlessness, everything was connected to everything else. I heard a great translucency and transparency of sound, every voice sounded with exquisite precision; and I heard something which is really difficult to define, but a rapturous inner poetry that connected everything. And these are the qualities that I hear in your playing. So when I first heard you play, without knowing that you'd been Clifford's pupil, I was thinking of Clifford Curzon because I was experiencing through your playing, fifty years later, what I'd experienced listening to him as a young man.

Seymour: This is so interesting. Were you amazed when you heard that I studied with him?

Andrew: It was amazing, but looking back at it, it isn't surprising, because I think one of the most extraordinary things that happens in a real creative life is that beings who have a destiny together meet each other to help each other. And that these beings are brought together through deep secret aspects of their temperament.

Seymour: Fascinating, fascinating.

Andrew: My great teachers have all been like that, and I won't go into all of them, but the man who was my Clifford Curzon was a great Benedictine mystic called Father Bede Griffiths. He was the greatest Christian mystic of the twentieth century. I met him in his eighties, and we had the most transformative relationship.

Seymour: Oh, how wonderful.

Andrew: Bede and I were superficially very, very different people, but we were linked by so many things, so many aspects of our temperament that have become clearer as the years go by.

Seymour: Beautiful.

Andrew: So it had to be him for me, just as it had to be Clifford for you because of these subtle inner connections—what Goethe calls "elective affinities," affinities of vision or passion or temperament, or all three, which mysteriously attract to us the people who resonate with them and so can help us live them more richly and evolve them more profoundly. Getting back to Clifford, I'd love to know how the relationship unfolded. Did you always manage to heal the difficulties in his interactions, or was there a time where you had to really separate from him?

Seymour: Life with him eventually became very difficult, for personal reasons. The problem became serious enough for me to consult with my psychologist friend: "I have to decide whether to break this relationship, and forfeit the greatest musical training that I ever had, or to put up with it for the sake of what I derive musically from this man." I decided on the second, because I couldn't live without the musical inspiration that I got from Clifford. I then had to put up with his very difficult emotional problems.

Andrew: Even given what you had to suffer from Clifford, it's clear he gave you priceless gifts. What is it that you acquired from him? What vision of pianism comes to you when you think of him?

Seymour: Andrew, you used a striking phrase in your question, "vision of pianism." Clifford seemed possessed of visions as he played. Perhaps it would be more accurate to say that they were "visions of beauty." He tried always to forget that he was playing a mechanical instrument. In fact he was the only pianist I knew who insisted that the music desk remain in the piano during performances. I once asked him about this, and he replied that he disliked having to see the hammers and dampers move inside the piano while he was performing. In short, his vision was to transform a percussive instrument into a vocal one. It resulted in an intricate shaping of phrases, but not like saying or thinking "Now, this note is a little louder, and this note is even louder than that one, and now the next note is a little softer." One could draw a graph after you decide how to phrase something, and as an afterthought you could change your mind about the shaping. But how you come to that decision, is what is crucial here. When Clifford and I would come to decisions like that, it was what I said before: the music told us that it needs to do something in particular.

That in turn brings up another major issue. Pitches can go higher or lower, right? Usually, when pitches go higher, they want to get louder. Both Clifford and I always had the instinct in almost all cases to pull away from high tones. Once I heard Clifford tell a pupil in Fontainebleau, "You have to rise with the difficulty. You can't get to the high note so easily. You have to pretend it's very difficult to reach, as it would be for a singer." It's what I said before: we both felt music in our vocal chords. As a matter of fact, Clifford actually let out vocal sounds. He would emit a "tsssssss," or a "chhhhhhhh," for that very reason. You know, all the greatest pianists have always suggested that we imitate singers when phrasing.

But unfortunately, we can't make crescendos and diminuendos on a single tone as singers do. Clifford used to say often, "Playing beautifully on the piano requires illusions. We can create the illusion of a crescendo on a long tone by making the crescendo with the accompanying figures while gently moving our torso towards the keyboard."

Andrew: Magicians, you are.

Seymour: And now, Andrew, we come to profound sadness. One day I heard that Clifford was very sick with a blood disorder. I was alarmed, and phoned him.

"Clifford, are you sick?"

"Oh yes, Seymour, I'm very sick, I have a blood disease." He added, "Why are you calling me? Are you afraid I'm going to die?"

I said, "Yes."

"Well," he replied in an attempt to be cheerful, "we all have to die, laddie."

There was something ominous in his reply. I knew the situation was serious. He died shortly after that on September 1, 1982. He was seventy-five.

Andrew: But one of the stories I love most is the story of how you may very well have gotten him his knighthood. Do tell me that one.

Seymour: Oh, this was so charming, well—

Andrew: Because he died *Sir* Clifford Curzon, after all.

Seymour: Yes, and this meant a great deal to him. One day, I penned a letter to Queen Elizabeth. I never wrote to a queen before, so I didn't know how to address the letter. I wrote, "Dear Your Majesty." But I understand it would have been proper to say "Your Majesty." Or "Madam." Isn't that correct, Andrew?

Andrew: I'm not sure. I must brush up on my palace etiquette.

Seymour: After that, I wrote, "Those of us in America wonder why Clifford Curzon hasn't been knighted along with all the distinguished English artists that have been knighted. We in America adore his playing," and so forth. I signed my name and I addressed it, "Queen Elizabeth, Buckingham Palace, London." It was just on a whim. I wondered if the letter would ever find its way to the queen. Around Christmastime, all sorts of interesting envelopes were stuffed into my mailbox. I saw an impressive one, though, a beautiful white envelope with a red coat of arms of lions on the back. *Wow,* I thought, *somebody is sending me a very fancy Christmas card.* I opened it up, and this is what it said: "Her Majesty the Queen has commanded me to send your letter to the Prime Minister." It was signed by Queen Elizabeth's secretary. I was dumbstruck! My letter was taken seriously. One month later, Clifford called me to say that he had been knighted. If he knew that I had anything to do with it, he would have erected a guillotine in Lincoln Center and beheaded me. Whether my letter instigated the knighting, or whether it was just a coincidence can't be confirmed.

Andrew: It's a beautiful story because it shows the pupil in a wild act, calling out to the universe to celebrate his teacher and the universe responding. I love it.

Seymour: I know; I love it too.

3.

THE EVERYDAY
PRACTICE OF
TEACHING

Andrew: Seymour, tell me a little about the experience of teaching. How is it for you day in and day out? Does it become a drain? Are you stressed by the daily demands on you by your students?

Seymour: Many of my colleagues tell me that when they finish a day of teaching, they're gone, they're spent. They're ready to go to bed. I say, "Really. I'm fresher when I finish teaching than when I started. I have more energy, and feel more alive. I'm ready for more dancing." And that's because I get such a joy out of helping my pupils feel good about themselves. When they go out of my door, I can see they're quite different from the person that came in. They've had a revelatory experience and they have more confidence in themselves, and they have enjoyed an hour and a half of being loved, unconditionally, only with the desire to make them better, to accept their faults, but mostly to stress their assets. To build upon what's already there. So that makes me feel fresh at the end of the day.

I can't say every day because not every pupil is so responsive, and occasionally I have had to dismiss certain pupils. I can't penetrate them, I can't change them, and they're going to detract from what it is that I do.

Andrew: So really you have to be very discerning as a teacher. You have to be first of all humble enough to realize that however gifted you are as a teacher, you won't be able to teach everyone.

Seymour: Of course.

Andrew: The second thing you really have to be aware of is that some people who come to you may have a dark agenda, even unconscious to them, but you've got to be conscious of it because it could in subtle ways destroy your gifts, and destroy the gifts that you have to give to others.

Seymour: Well there you are, so self-protection has to come into play here.

Andrew: And how, Seymour, do you who are so expansive and loving, protect yourself? What are the strategies that you use for self-protection?

Seymour: When I give my best to a pupil, and they don't return the goodness that I'm offering them, I get alarmed and I wait from lesson to lesson to see if there's going to be some change, some indication that they're appreciative of what I'm doing for them. I do believe that in any relationship, anything other than reciprocity is obscene. One cannot be a giver without being a receiver, and vice versa.

Andrew: You have to have a dance partner in other words.

Seymour: Yes. We have to choreograph together. When I can't get that to happen, I have to have a parting of the ways. In one case, in all the years that I've been teaching, now let's add it up. I started when I was fifteen, and I'm now eighty-eight, and by the way, I'm teaching more than ever now. So what is from fifteen to eighty-eight?

Andrew: It's seventy-three years. If I asked you at eighty-eight to name one really extraordinary metamor-phosis you've seen in somebody who's been your pupil from being very shy and distraught to being very awake and abandoned—

Seymour: Richard Shirk.

Andrew: Ah, tell me about him.

Seymour: Oh, it's so sad, he died. He had tinnitus, and they operated to sever a nerve in the ear, and while he was in the hospital, they killed him. They accidentally gave him the wrong medication, and he became a vegetable and died.

When he first came to me, he was a total wreck. Although he was extremely gifted, he couldn't disci-pline himself to practice. I had performing classes once a month for my pupils: "Richard, I want you to play the first movement of your Beethoven concerto." Now we're at the class. "Richard, it's time for you to play now."

"No, I'm not ready."

Next month, "Richard, I have your favorite chocolate for you. If you play me the first movement of your Beethoven concerto, I'll give you the chocolate. If you won't play, you can't have the chocolate."

He played.

Andrew: Wonderful.

Seymour: I found out he loved a certain kind of salami that he bought in Zabar's. So I went to Zabar's and bought a quarter pound of this salami. I lured him with it in the next class: "Do you know what I have in the kitchen for you? Play me the Chopin Fantasie, and you'll get your favorite salami." He played the Chopin Fantasie. I nurtured him like this with false rewards.

And then, the best thing happened. He entered the Leschetizky debut contest and won it. The prize was a debut in Tully Hall. He was very neurotic, and by this time he took everything that I taught him and converted it into such detail that I could no longer answer his questions. For example, he was going to begin his debut with Beethoven's Sonata Op. 110. It opens with a four-voice chord. He called me up, once every hour with "It is true, isn't it, that the top voice should be the loudest."

I said, "Absolutely."

One hour later: "Well, are the bass and the tenor the same volume, or is the tenor less than the bass?"

I said, "Richard, I don't even know what the answer to that is. It seems to me that the other voices are all soft."

"You mean they're all the same dynamic?" he said quite upset.

"Richard, you're going too far, you're going to analyze Op. 110 out of existence. Just stop this."

The concert was a brilliant success. He developed into one of the most formidable pianists that you could ever imagine. I typed him from the very beginning as being unmusical, and I thought that I would have to stimulate every phrase for his entire life. But in time he brought me new repertoire, which he performed with natural expression. I helped to draw out the deepest musicality in him.

Andrew: So something awoke in him through this long process.

Seymour: I removed some barriers that suffocated his natural musical instincts. They could have been psychological, they could have been physical, they could have been mental, they could have been all three. I have no idea what happened, but suddenly he became a natural, expressive pianist. Everyone in my circle, and in his circle, recognized this. He was formidable, and a most marvelous teacher; his pupils adored him. And he goes and dies on us. I was grief-stricken.

Andrew: One thing we've talked about a lot is how sad it is that many musicians don't approach the making of music with this vision.

Seymour: That's true. They do it mechanically. And then there is something of the showmanship of sitting at the piano and playing music in front of people: "Look what I can do." There are a lot of performers who just thrive on applause, and the fact that they're attracting huge numbers of people. They have the feeling that the audience is filled with people who have assembled to honor them.

Now I'm going to make a general statement: many people don't do things for the right reasons. For example, I have pupils who graduate from college. I ask them what their plans are.

"I'm going to go for my master's," one says.

"Why are you going for your master's?"

"Oh, well, I can't get a good job unless I do."

"And what makes you think that you'll get a good job even with your master's? Don't you know what the competition is like? Even with a Ph.D. degree you're up against five hundred people or more applying for a job in a small university in some unknown city. Is that what you want to do in life?"

If a pupil would say to me, "I want to go for my master's because I want to continue developing my mind," I would say, "Bravo for you." But to cite the possibility of a larger salary as the only reason for getting a degree is self-destructiveness acting itself out to the fullest degree.

Andrew: I want to get back to the sadness of musicians not realizing that in making music they are actually transforming themselves and learning how to dance with the mystery of life.

Seymour: Yes.

Andrew: Many of the greatest pianists have been deeply disturbed people, very un-integrated people; and in the film you talk a great deal about Glenn Gould because for you it's clear that Glenn Gould, although a genius, sums up everything that you think is wrong about playing.

Seymour: I do. But in my opinion he's an example of someone whose neurotic nature affected his playing. You know that he has a huge following. They're ready to attack me. At some of the Q & A sessions, in different parts of the country, and especially in Canada, some of the people in the audience took me to task: "Why do you say those things about Glenn Gould? I find his Bach illuminating."

I said, "I find your response interesting, but don't you agree that we all have our own response to individual artists? And sadly I do not find his Bach illuminating."

And the man sat down.

Now let's discuss whether Glenn Gould's neurotic nature adversely affects his playing, or if his neurotic playing adversely affects his nature? Perhaps they go hand in hand. In the documentary Ethan mentioned great artists in music and in acting who are monsters in their personal lives. He wondered if there is something in extraordinary talent that adversely affects the psyche. Shall I tell you about another person who fits this category?

Andrew: Yes.

Seymour: Clifford Curzon.

Andrew: Absolutely.

Seymour: He was a supreme artist and a wreck of a human being. This is what I think: I believe that the process of integrating into your personal life all the positive components necessary to become a great artist doesn't always happen naturally. Most artists have consciously to pay attention to the process and manually, so to speak, direct hard-earned artistic accomplishments into their everyday lives. There are difficulties here: some artists don't even know that it's possible, while other artists like Clifford Curzon don't wish to do that. In fact when I told

Sir Clifford that I was writing *With Your Own Two Hands* and that it was a book that suggests that productive practicing and performing can make us not only into better musicians, but, more importantly, into better people, he remarked, "How interesting, laddie. I try to keep my art uncontaminated from my social world." In other words, he was working to bring about the very demarcation that I was suggesting you avoid. Ideally, there should be no difference between Clifford Curzon the artist, and Clifford Curzon the man.

Andrew: Clearly he was terrified by aspects of his personality and wanting to protect Clifford the artist from Clifford the person.

Seymour: But it never occurred to him that Clifford the artist could ameliorate and harmonize Clifford the person. This is what my book is about. I think that's what the documentary is about.

Andrew: Why do you think people have no idea of this?

Seymour: I can't account for that. There's one example after another of the most neurotic people who are supreme artists. And Ethan mentioned some of them, including actors.

Andrew: And part of the deep meaning of your life has been to incarnate this integration of art and life. I think this is one of the deep reasons why you left the concert stage, because at a certain level you must have known that had you continued in that life it would have devastated you and made you extremely neurotic, so you might have continued to play extremely well, but your life would have been destroyed.

Seymour: I can tell you right now: if I continued pursuing a solo career, I would have been dead long ago. That's what a strain it was for me. I wouldn't have minded the strain; as I said in the documentary, "I would go to war for my art." But what I couldn't bear is the hypocrisy of the commercial world and managers who live off the talent of others. I couldn't stand that whole scenario; it was intolerable to me.

Andrew: But it leads to the question: Do you think that this kind of integration we're talking about can be attained within the lunatic asylum of fame and celebrity?

Seymour: I do think so. If the artists knew that it was possible.

Andrew: Have you seen it?

Seymour: Have I seen what?

Andrew: Have you seen famous musicians with happy, integrated personalities and lives?

Seymour: Anton Rubinstein had a very harmonious personal life. Yo-Yo Ma has a lovely life.

Andrew: Perfect choices. They are such lovely, generous, kind, and humble men, as well as being such magnificent musicians.

Seymour: Did you know that the former president of Sony, Mr. Ohga, was the only corporate president in the world who was a professional conductor? Through his secretary and my dear friend Hiroko Onoyama, I learned that Mr. Ohga and Yo-Yo Ma were going to perform the Dvorâk Concerto together. They wanted to have a rehearsal to discuss tempi and interpretive issues, and they needed a pianist to perform a reduction of the orchestral part. Hiroko asked me if I would be interested, and I told her I would love to do it. So I bought a copy of the piano reduction and the solo part. I learned it so thoroughly that I could have played Yo-Yo Ma's part myself. I knew every note. On the day that we were to get together, Yo-Yo Ma went to the hospital with pneumonia.

Andrew: So you missed—

Seymour: And we never did get together.

Andrew: But have you met him in person—

Seymour: Oh, and how. Whenever I meet him, he takes me around and almost crushes my ribs. He's so outgoing and warm.

Andrew: I've been at master classes that he's given and he's a teacher who, like you, makes his pupils glow with joy.

Seymour: He loves them.

Andrew: He loves them with his full being, and there's never a moment where he asks for admiration or pulls rank. He is entranced by the glory of teaching.

Seymour: He himself becomes a pupil. He becomes humble.

Andrew: I can think of another musician who really would believe the truth of what you're saying.

Seymour: And that is?

Andrew: Yehudi Menuhin.

Seymour: I didn't know him personally.

Andrew: I met Yehudi several times. He was an astoundingly beautiful person. He had a very deep and rich marriage. He was dedicated to Indian spirituality and to the pursuit of yoga—

Seymour: Yes, I know about that.

Andrew: Which he took as a way of consciously shaping his whole being to become the instrument of music. He was a very, very remarkable person.

Seymour: Did you know that he was one of the world's greatest prodigies?

Andrew: I did; I know his life story. He recorded the Elgar Violin Concerto with Elgar himself at thirteen. A year later, he became the surrogate son of the old and reclusive Willa Cather, and in his sixties and seventies pioneered the East-West fusion in music by working with the great sitarist Ravi Shankar. He had an amazingly full and bravely exploratory life. But what is more important even than being one of the world's great prodigies, and one of the world's great violinists, is that he lived a life dedicated to the whole of reality through music.

Seymour: Yes.

Andrew: I think another person would be Casals.

Seymour: He was very similar.

Andrew: I think Casals was not only a stupendous cellist, but a very fine being who understood the universal meaning of music and who devoted his whole life to becoming one with music in heart, mind, soul, and body, so that he could not only play music, but represent the soul of music in his being.

Seymour: Now I have two comments to make. One about Yehudi Menuhin, who lived very close to Clifford Curzon. Clifford would tell me that Yehudi would stand on his head in a yoga position, and Clifford thought that was very injurious to the little bones in the neck. So he didn't approve of that. But Yehudi Menuhin, at the age of twelve, played the Beethoven Concerto with the New York Philharmonic. No child prodigy ever played the Beethoven Violin Concerto because you don't associate that particular piece with a child prodigy. It's far too deep for a child to comprehend. Yet, at the end of Menuhin's performance, every member of the orchestra was crying.

Now the story goes that George Enescu, his teacher, never taught Yehudi the basics of violin playing because Yehudi was completely natural. And so when Yehudi became a teenager, he asked himself one day, *I wonder how I do that.* Well, he didn't know how and why he played so well. He became self-conscious, and his playing deteriorated until he died. That is, it deteriorated from the standard that he had enjoyed as a child prodigy. He even started to play a little out of tune, and it was very sad. I think that he was searching for some way out of this dilemma with all the mystical training that he had, hoping it would help him. But what he really needed was sound musical instruction, which he never got.

Andrew: What a sad story.

Seymour: Yes it is. And then there is a story about Casals. He, like a surprising number of performers, had ambivalence about performing. According to what he wrote in his biography, he was caught in an avalanche in his twenties and a stone pinned his left hand against the mountain. It was at the height of his career. In his autobiography he wrote something like this: "Thank God I won't have to perform in public again."

Andrew: I think that most of the great performers had ambivalent feelings about performing.

Seymour: I think you're right. With a story like Casals' the truth finally came out. The same with stage fright. Years ago, no one spoke about it out of shame. Now it's common knowledge because great performers have written about it. Look how Ethan came out about it in the documentary. Bravo for him.

Andrew: Yes.

Seymour: I know the former manager of one of the world's greatest pianists. He told me, "You would not believe what goes on before he goes out on the stage. He has to lie down, and someone has to massage his back. He's a wreck."

Andrew: I met Cecil Beaton before he died, and he told me about how Maria Callas had invited him to be in the wings when she was singing *Medea* in Covent Garden. And he thought, *Why is Maria asking me to be in the wings?* Well, he found out because just before Medea was meant to enter the opera, he saw this shivering woman standing next to him. And he realized with a shock that that was Callas and she was about to go on, and what she said to him shivering and shaking was, "I can't go on, I can't go on, push me."

Seymour: Whoa.

Andrew: So Cecil Beaton told me that he had to push Callas, and he said it was the strangest moment of his life because one moment she'd been this helpless, bloody mess of nerves. When he pushed her, he saw the most uncanny transformation take place in front of his eyes. One minute later her arms were outstretched, the chords of her entrance as Medea were being sounded, and this woman had become transformed into this terrifying shamanic presence.

Callas is unfortunately not a good example of your thesis because although she was the greatest of artists, she was destroyed psychologically from a very early age and suffered horribly and died tragically. I think this vision that you have of learning to become an integrated being through music is a kind of prayer. It's something that you know has happened to you, and you know that it's possible. And you've seen in a few great artists that this has happened, but you've also seen in thousands of pupils, in thousands of artists, that it hasn't happened. So it's very rare, let's face it, that it truly comes to fruition.

Seymour: As long as it can happen, then it's possible.

Andrew: Let's go for it. As long as it can happen, we should really strive for it.

Seymour: Of course.

Andrew: Yes.

Seymour: It's the reason for teaching. You can't save everyone, but you have to make the attempt. I think that a person like me imbued with so many riches must share them with others. Otherwise they will atrophy within me.

4.

THE DANCE

Andrew: Finally, I'd love to concentrate on what I find the most inspiring aspect of your vision of teaching: that learning how to play an instrument is learning how to play life with your full being.

Seymour: That's exactly right. It is learning how to play life.

Andrew: That to me is a revelation. It is what I myself have experienced in learning the piano and in loving music all of these years. I've never played for you and if I did, you'd discover that my piano playing is like my Italian, exuberant but inaccurate. Even so, there are times when I'm battling through a simple Mozart or Bach piece when, quite suddenly, I feel myself come into unity in heart, body, mind, and soul with the music and I know that this is how I should live my whole life with my whole being harmonized and concentrated on whatever is unfolding. But until I met you, I never met anyone who lived this awareness so completely and who understood it so radically. So, Seymour, how did you yourself come to understand this?

Seymour: Well, I believe that this vision began within me while I paid deep attention to my responses during my practicing. I remember something that a very successful professional writer friend once said to me: "Writing is not a way of life for me. It is life." I would like to replace her word *writing* with the word *music* and say with full conviction that music *is* life. Why is it life? Well, it incorporates everything that constitutes a healthy person. Through productive practicing and performing we can achieve an integration of our spiritual, emotional, and intellectual worlds within the framework of a healthy functioning body. It's no different than what psychologists tell us: a healthy person is someone whose emotional and intellectual worlds are integrated within the framework of a healthy functioning body.

So now I'm working on a piece of music, and the first thing that I believe one does is to respond emotionally, because music basically is a language of feeling. Well now, I respond emotionally and then I see innumerable notational indications written down by the composer. Tenuto here, please. That means, "Don't gradually go slower, but slow down the tempo right then and there." If I don't do that, I'm not obeying and coming close to what the composer was feeling when he wrote down that measure. So there my intellect comes into play. And now feeling and thinking are synthesized. I can't tell which one is more important because they're no longer separated.

Andrew: You can't really tell which is your feeling and which is your mind because they're working together in service of the music.

Seymour: They're synthesized.

Andrew: Dancing together.

Seymour: The word *synthesized* is the best word. They're synthesized. And so now I'm trying to coax an inanimate object to reproduce this. You can just imagine what that's like. There are eighty-eight keys, white and black ones, and you depress a key and a hammer is flung to a string at a certain rate of speed. The faster it is propelled to the string, the louder the sound; the slower it is propelled, the softer the sound. Now you can just imagine we're dealing with ten fingers, and each finger is a personality unto itself. And then they have to be all synthesized so that there aren't ten fingers any longer, but one concept that comes from the meeting place of ten fingers.

You don't actually think about that as a pianist. I mean I'm just saying that out loud as an afterthought of what the process is. So when you get to know your instrument, you have to make a physical connection so that the keys really do go down and the hammers are really propelled at the exact rate of speed that's going to coincide with your synthesized feeling and thinking. That's why we practice.

And now, what is a primary requirement of that? We have to thank Chopin for the answer, because before he died, he began to compile a piano method. He was a supremely gifted teacher. Knowing his music, what do you suppose he thought was the chief requirement for learning to perform music on the piano? I would think it would be "Everything depends on playing poetically," or "Everything depends on a beautiful tone." But here is what Chopin wrote: "Everything depends on the correct fingering."

Now you stop and say, "Why did he think that?" The reason is, if you're not comfortable on the keyboard, there's no way you can play with expression. If you don't have the right fingering, you can't get through to synthesized feeling and thinking. And since all hands are different, instrumentalists must come up with their own fingering. And finally comes the coordination of both feet on the pedals. Arthur Rubinstein said it best. He referred to the right pedal as "the soul of the piano." So all of this goes into practicing and communicating with pupils, leading them into the heart-center of the music. As you said, it's no different than the life process.

Andrew: And no different than the spiritual training that I have done for forty years in my privacy. I practice every single day, and many times a day, the mantras that I love, the visualizations that I have adored. And I practice them to stay in a stream of spacious, clear, lucid, tender, compassionate awareness. Because I know that if I stay in that compassionate, lucid awareness that is so boundless, then whatever happens during my day, I will be able to rise to it and make music out of it instead of being made scrambled eggs by it. Just as in great music there are difficult passages that demand disciplined and repeated attention, so in any life devoted to the rigor of spiritual practice, difficulties and resistances will arise and overwhelm you unless you're dogged and persist humbly in asking for, and working with, the grace to pass through them.

Seymour: Yes. In other words, you won't be a victim any longer.

Andrew: No. I'll be dancing with reality instead of being crushed or maimed or distorted by reality.

Seymour: I noticed that you use the word *dancing* very often.

Andrew: Yes.

Seymour: Could you explain to me why you use the word *dancing*?

Andrew: For me—

Seymour: Do you believe that you and I are dancing together?

Andrew: Yes.

Seymour: Is it like a rapport that exists between two people, and/or between you and a particular experience that you're trying to bring into yourself?

Andrew: Seymour, I must tell you the truth: for me the divine is a dancer, and the greatest image of the divine comes from the part of India that I was born in, where God is represented as a dancer with the flame of destruction in one hand and the drum of creation in the other.

Seymour: Oh, you mean this is a religious icon?

Andrew: Yes, it's called Shiva Nataraja, the king— the raja—of the dance. In the great sculptures of south India that the old sages called Shiva's dancing ground, the divine is represented as a beautiful, elegant, athletic young man in a dance pose with four hands. In the right upper hand, he holds the drum of creation, in the left the flame of destruction. The lower right hand extends in a gesture of eternal protection; the relaxed lower left arm gestures at his right foot, symbolizing the endless grace the god of the dance pours out to those who adore him. His right foot meanwhile is shown trampling a dwarf that represents the limited selfish ego. The great Christian mystic Nicholas of Cusa said that "God is a coincidence of opposites," and in this representation of Shiva Nataraja we find, I believe, the most complete and thrilling image of the paradoxical qualities and powers of the divine.

Seymour: I've heard about this but didn't know its full significance.

Andrew: My deepest devotion is to God as dancer. In the Acts of John, an apocryphal text long known in fragments, Jesus is actually described dancing at the last supper, asking the disciples to dance. In this astounding gnostic text you'll find this written: "Before he was arrested . . . Jesus assembled us all and said, 'Let us sing a song to the Father and go to meet what lies before us.' So he told us to form a circle, holding one another's hands. Jesus stood in the middle . . ."

Seymour: And danced? Really?

Andrew: Yes. Jesus and the disciples danced before Jesus went through the agony of the crucifixion and the resurrection.

Seymour: Is that so, they actually danced?

Andrew: Yes, and while dancing, Jesus sings out something that has become my secret credo. He says in the Acts of John, "The universe belongs to the dancer. If you do not dance, you do not know what is happening."

Seymour: And what did he specifically mean by dance?

Andrew: Everybody who understands God as dancer means the following: life itself is a dance of opposites, light and dark, the universe is a constant dance of matter and light—

Seymour: You mean movement.

Andrew: Movement and stasis. Light and matter. Light and dark. All of these opposites are dancing.

Seymour: So dance is really a metaphor.

Andrew: It's more than a metaphor; it's the ultimate reality. Now we have quantum physics describing how the energy of light works, very much like a dance. So the universe is a dance, life is a dance; and if you're going to truly awaken fully and completely, you must be able to dance with the different aspects of life, and you must also bring the whole of yourself, body, heart, mind, into the enthusiasm and beauty and dynamism of the dance. So why I love this image is because dancing requires the whole of you. And if you're going to truly live an awake life, it requires the whole of you being lit up by love, passion, courage, and intelligence. And one of the reasons why I love so much your vision of music is that when you describe sitting at a piano with your mind focused on the truth of the structures of the music, your heart open to the glorious messages that the music is giving, and with your body trained—

Seymour: The brain, don't leave out the brain.

Andrew: I said mind, I said brain.

Seymour: Yes.

Andrew: Wait, wait, let me finish—and your body trained, what you're describing is the discipline of a dancer.

Seymour: I see that now.

Andrew: So the pianist is dancing with the music, with the deep sacred intentions of the composer, and in order to be able to dance, you have to have extraordinary abandon coupled with extraordinary discipline, you have to marry those opposites.

Seymour: You have to allow it to happen, and then observe what's happening so that it becomes conscious to you, and not interfere when it's happening. Just allow it to happen. That's my process. I just allow it to happen. I go with my initial instincts, and then I pay attention to what they are as an afterthought.

Andrew: So let's get back to your teaching. You're helping people to become dancers in this way, dancers with music.

Seymour: As a matter of fact, dancers specifically do all of these things.

Andrew: They do, I know.

Seymour: They're moved by an emotional response, and their mind teaches them what part of the body is going to be activated, and how it's going to be activated. It's not unlike playing an instrument.

Andrew: No, it's the same. They're playing their own instrument.

Seymour: Their body is their instrument.

Andrew: Yes. But when I watch you play, I am looking at a dancer. A calm, wise, surrendered dancer. Your whole being, your body, your mind, your soul, your heart, are all dancing with this invisible world that is music.

Seymour: Would you like to know something very interesting? You know my book *With Your Own Two Hands*? Do you know what the heart of the book is? It's called "Choreography at the Piano."

Andrew: Yes.

Seymour: Dancing.

Andrew: Yes.

Seymour: And I describe it. I say, "We're in a sense dancers. Every movement that we make is a dance. Our fingers, our wrists, our arm, our body, our legs, at the pedal—we have to make the right choreographic movements or what we're feeling and thinking won't come out." So I use the word *choreography* at the piano. Little did I know that I would meet someone who would teach me that in the spiritual world, and in the mystic world, god is dancing.

Andrew: Energy—God is consciousness energy. Light consciousness energy. That light consciousness energy is dancing to create absolutely everything that exists out of itself. And it dances to sustain the life that it's danced out of itself. And it's dancing on an unbelievably massive scale with all the different opposites dancing together.

Seymour: Would you say that it's the microcosm of the macrocosm?

Andrew: Yes.

Seymour: That the universe is dancing.

Andrew: The whole universe is dancing.

Seymour: So we're the microcosm of it.

Andrew: Yes. And that's what is so moving to me about the way in which you teach. What you're really teaching is of course an amazingly precise way of truly communicating the essence of music. But you're teaching something even more important than that, you're teaching how to dance with reality, how to come into a lucid, spontaneous, disciplined abandon that enables you to respond subtly and immediately to whatever arises. That is mastery. That's mastery that the Dalai Lama would recognize, that the Buddha would recognize, that Jesus would recognize, that Ramakrishna would recognize as the goal of human life. So this is why we're sitting on this sofa: because in our different but deeply unified ways it's this integration that we have been pursuing—you have pursued it with such beauty and integrity and passion through your dedication to music, and I have pursued it through my dedication to mystical practice, and a vision of the radiant integration it can make possible.

Seymour: It comes out the same because we're both aiming for the same thing.

Andrew: It's the same reality that we're celebrating. You call it the reservoir; I can call it whatever I want. Names are not important. What is important is the dance.

Seymour: Exactly.

Andrew: What is important is keeping this vibrant, subtle, tender, lucid energy always arising in us. So that we can live the fullest of our lives, experience the depth of our talent, love the heaven out of our friends, enjoy the agonies and ecstasies of reality itself. We need to be able to live dancing, and make our death our last dance. There's a wonderful poem by Rumi when he says, "One day in your wine shop, I drank a little wine, and I threw off the robe of my body and I knew, drunk on you, this creation is harmony. Creation, destruction, I am dancing for them both." Well, a very great pianist playing the *Hammerklavier* is playing a monumental, cosmic dance in sound, and has to be a dancer that can transmit all of the electric steps of that dance.

Seymour: I see.

Andrew: And in order to be that dancer, the pianist will have to not only evolve in all the ways that you're describing, but also to be a truly great interpreter of what Beethoven is communicating, will have to enter the naked, fierce field of the dance of reality itself, and comprehend why Beethoven is stretching all of the powers of music to be able to begin to convey this massive, cosmic ballet of opposites. Isn't that it?

Seymour: Even the act of playing one note, the first note of a piece on the piano is a kind of dance involving subtle contrasting movements in the arms and hands. When I was in Martha's Vineyard, I gave a master class to two adult pianists. One of them was a professional pianist, the other was an amateur. Both played extremely well. I observed these pianists musically and physically. Both of them placed their fingers on the first notes of their pieces and pushed the keys down. I call it harpooning a note. I then went into a detailed description of how to depress the first tones of any piece.

There is a scientific law: anything that is set in motion must have a preparatory swing stroke in the opposite direction. Let's take golf: the golf ball has to be propelled away from you. Therefore, the golf club must first swing behind you with the exact speed necessary to project the ball. If the ball is to be driven a long distance, the swing stroke must be faster; the opposite if you plan simply to putt the ball a short distance. The preparatory stroke is slower. It's a dance of a kind with very subtle choreography in the arms and hands and fingers.

Now, for piano keys. Everything works in contrary motion on the piano: you depress a key and a hammer goes up; you depress the right pedal and the dampers go up. If you wish to play a loud sound on the piano, you place your finger on the surface of the key with a low wrist. Now you swing your wrist up with a fast motion and swoosh it down with a fast motion, thereby lowering the key at a fast rate of speed. This transfers energy to the hammer and propels it up to the strings at a fast rate of speed, producing a loud sound. The opposite takes place for a soft sound, namely the preparatory swing is slower. The important thing to remember is that the sound is programmed in the speed of the preparatory swing stroke.

Andrew: Beyond all of this knowledge of specific technique which is so important, there's a mystery to playing at the core of it all which can never be exhausted.

Seymour: So true. However and whatever techniques we are taught, we end up self-motivated, searching for the truth within ourselves, pulling out the real secrets from our *spiritual reservoir*. All the secrets are there. And we have to be humble, and learn from our mentors as much as we can, but we can't admonish them for not teaching us everything because they can't. So the rest of the time we have to teach ourselves. In fact all the serious performers I have spoken to admit that their teachers could only take them to a certain point, and they figured out the rest.

Andrew: The most important thing that I've learned about teaching is that the great teachers model how to learn. When I sit with the Dalai Lama, I am of course deeply awed by him, humbled by him, moved by him to my depths. I try to drink in his essence with every pore of my body and soul and heart and mind because I truly love him beyond any words that I can use. But what moves me the most about him is his own constant commitment in the deepest humility to learning what he's teaching, and in the end that's what he communicates to me most completely.

Seymour: Yes.

Andrew: And I am able to learn from him only if I have a comparable commitment, a comparable sincerity, a comparable transparence, a comparable honesty, a comparable deep humor.

Seymour: Wonderful.

Andrew: What did Clifford Curzon transmit to you? I believe he modeled for you something that was already vibrant in you—a commitment to go on learning how to shape phrases in such a way as to elevate people by their beauty and truth.

Seymour: What I learned most from him was watching him at the keyboard. The sound that he drew from the piano was a model for me to work towards. I had then to figure out how to reproduce that sound choreographically through certain dance movements. Otherwise, it's just not going to come out of the piano. So you have to be really honest with yourself and listen to what is coming out of the piano. I always tell my pupils, "You know, we're very much like ventriloquists. We're sitting at the keyboard, and we're depressing keys at different rates of speed. But the sound is coming out a few feet away from us where the hammers are being propelled to the strings, and the dampers are going up and down. Your ear has to be focused there, and not at the keyboard. Physically, you're at the keyboard, but as a ventriloquist your ear is where the dummy's mouth is. Do you follow that, Andrew?

Andrew: I do. As a last question, what would you love to communicate to all teachers?

Seymour: Number one: you're not teaching pupils, you're teaching people. Number two: the most important thing that you can do for your pupils is to make them emotionally responsive not only to everything in music, but more importantly, to every aspect of life. That is primary. Everything else will come after that.

And what would you, Andrew, say to those who are called to be spiritual teachers?

Andrew: Learn first how to dance your own life beautifully to the music of divine reality, as beautifully and with as much sacred discipline and compassion as you can, and then what you teach will pulse with the rhythm of Shiva Nataraja, God the dancer. As a great devotee of Shiva, India's Rumi, Manikkavacakar, once wrote, "Teach me, oh beloved, the steps of your dance so I can share them with others humbly, so I, and they, together, can be danced by you."

CODA:
Reverence For Life

Andrew: Seymour, I've been with you now for a week, eating with you, having hours of off-duty silliness with you, exploring so many of life's aspects with you.

Yesterday you touched me deeply by the way you treated the shy and kind postmistress in your local post office. She was going through a difficult ordeal, and suddenly confided in you with me standing by and listening. You attended to her with such exquisite courtesy, dropping everything—although we had other chores to do before getting back to work—to listen to her and respond to her. You didn't say much; you just gazed at her with love, and took her hands, and patted her shoulder, and showed by the way you were with her how much you respected and liked her, and understood and commiserated with her suffering. When we left, I turned and looked back at her; she was almost literally glowing with peace and self-acceptance.

That scene kept coming back to me last night as I tried to get to sleep. For a long time I didn't understand why I was so haunted by its ordinary, extraordinary beauty, and then it came to me. At this stage of your life, you approach everything you do—from tidying your room, to cooking a marvelous chicken dinner for me, to teaching, to watching the sea—with what I can only call "reverence for life." The years have made you so attuned to your *spiritual reservoir*, so at home in it and with it, that you're at ease and at home with the whole world, and able naturally to reach out to whoever is in front of you with instinctual healing grace.

And then I understood something else that links us both deeply. Both of us are profoundly skeptical about organized religion because of the ways in which it can program people and condone horrific acts of exclusion, prejudice, and violence. And yet our skepticism about organized religion hasn't driven us away from what I call the divine and you call the *spiritual reservoir*. On the contrary, for both of us our disillusionment with manmade dogma has driven us deeper into a direct connection with, and reverence for, a constantly unfolding mystery that transcends always all the names and definitions humans can give it.

Seymour: When I contemplate the miracle of life, and the fact that the universe continues to expand, I fall on my knees in awe and wonderment. Certainly something is responsible for this. Yet, I consider it an affront when people give this force a name. For me, it transcends names. As I humble myself before it, I firmly believe that it is not given to me to know the answer to such a profound mystery. To accept this, to know unequivocally that there are no answers to certain questions, defines, in my estimation, the essence of *humility*.

Andrew: I love what Rumi wrote: "Real lovers serve the mystery in an ecstasy of humility." For me, those words enshrine the highest, most inspiring, truth. Seymour, do you believe in God?

Seymour: One day, a friend, who found my views on religion to be intolerable, approached me with the following question: "Conceive the vastness of the universe, galaxy upon galaxy, in an unmeasurable and endless space. How do you think that came about? Wouldn't you say that some intelligence created it, and controls it?"

I upset him with my familiar reply: "It beats me."

When people explain such a phenomenon in terms of a god, or any explanation at all, I feel offended. Why is it that people cannot accept that certain things cannot be explained?

Albert Einstein wrote:

> I cannot conceive of a God who rewards and punishes his creatures, or has a will of the kind that we experience in ourselves. Neither can I nor would I want to conceive of an individual that survives his physical death; let feeble souls, from fear or absurd egoism, cherish such thoughts. I am satisfied with the mystery of the eternity of life and with the awareness and a glimpse of the marvelous structure of the existing world, together with the devoted striving to comprehend a portion, be it ever so tiny, of the Reason that manifests itself in nature. (Albert Einstein, *The World As I See It* [New York: Philosophical Library, 1949], 11)

I also contemplate that some force governs the universe, a nameless, mysterious force, a power far beyond our comprehension. I feel that to name it is to demean it.

I could never conceive of bowing down in prayer. But I can bow down in wonder and in awe of the mystery of existence, of nature, and of the miraculous achievements of creative geniuses throughout the centuries. Humility does not allow me to explain, nor to give a name to these wonders. I am resigned never to find answers to certain questions. In fact, I consider my very existence to be the ultimate question mark.

Andrew: And yet you also know, Seymour, that each one of us is secretly connected, in our own unique way, to the *spiritual reservoir.*

Seymour: Of course, but what I have found is the more deeply we connect with it, the more the mystery of life expands and deepens. The more that we know, the more we realize how much we cannot know. And, so the more humble and reverent we are towards all beings and the universe itself, the more we can become enlightened.

Andrew: I feel so full of everything we've experienced together and expressed, I have nothing left to say, dear Seymour, but thank you and bless you.

Seymour: But there's something left to do. We've come to the end of our book and I would love to express my feeling of benediction not through words, but through music. There are so many things that can only be said with music. I'm going to play Bach, for Bach is for both of us the greatest of all composers. And for our dear readers, there is a link to YouTube on the last page so they can listen to this final musical benediction.

Andrew: Smiling, Seymour gets up off the sofa, walks slowly to the piano that stands in the corner of his living room in Maine, sits down, and begins to play a transcription from a Bach cantata called "God's Time Is Always the Best Time." He has played it for me once before, after one of our first magical dinners in New York, but now it is as if I am hearing it for the first time. I have never heard him, or anyone, play with such authority and sublime tenderness. Each note and chord unfolds inevitably, effortlessly, and with an ever-widening spaciousness, until the music seems to fill not only the room we are in, but, increasingly, the whole world around and beyond it. I know he is blessing not only me, our friendship, and the work we have done together, but himself, too, and the life of all beings everywhere. And when the last chord sounds, neither of us says a word. For one long, eternal moment, I, Seymour, the sun-drenched lawn and glittering sea outside, and the chipmunk munching almonds on the steps down to the garden, are one, at peace.

Seymour's final benediction:
https://www.youtube.com/watch?v=idREATkJrnc

ACKNOWLEDGMENTS

Andrew's acknowledgments:

To Shiva Nataraja, Lord of the Dance. To Patty Gift, soul-sister, great old friend, for believing and seeing this through. To Ned Leavitt, for his extraordinary generosity of soul and dazzling help. To Janet Thomas, for all her loving precision. To Anne Andrews, for her great sane wisdom and all her kindness. To Frances and Mike Cohoon, my Arkansas heart family, for their love. To Chaz Ebert, for herself, and her golden thumb. To Ellen Gunter, dear friend, for her diamantine and tireless work. And last but not least, to my beloved cat, Jade, for the joy she brings.

Seymour's acknowledgments:

To Patty Gift, Ned Leavitt, and the entire staff of Hay House,

Of course it takes a "village" to create a book. When I was told that the subtitle would be *Conversations with Seymour*, I knew that the distinguished scholar Andrew Harvey would be presenting questions to me, and that I would have to project words of wisdom. But now that I have read the book several times, I am convinced that Andrew's messages will carry a tremendous impact to all readers, whatever their age or occupation. I, myself, have learned an enormous amount from this extraordinary man.

As to the editing and publication of this book, I could never have imagined a team of professionals whose every contact with me was permeated with warmth, sensitivity, and care, similar to the way serious musicians turn a phrase of music. Patty Gift and Ned Leavitt were inspirations in themselves. Guiding me, encouraging me, correcting me, they were a vital source of the book's substance. And to all other members of the publishing staff, my heartfelt thanks for your help, always given with love and a deep sense of humanity.

ABOUT THE AUTHORS

Andrew Harvey is an internationally acclaimed poet, novelist, translator, mystical scholar and spiritual teacher. He has written and edited more than 30 books, including the bestselling titles *The Hope* and *The Tibetan Book of Living and Dying*. He has taught at Oxford University, Cornell University, Hobart and William Smith Colleges, the California Institute of Integral Studies, and the University of Creation Spirituality, as well as at various spiritual centres throughout the United States. He is the founder and director of the Institute for Sacred Activism.

www.andrewharvey.net

Seymour Bernstein is an American pianist, composer and teacher. He is the subject of the documentary *Seymour: An Introduction*, directed by the actor Ethan Hawke. One of the most sought-after workshop leaders and piano instructors in the United States and abroad, Mr Bernstein is also a prolific composer. His compositions range from teaching material for students of all levels to the most sophisticated concert pieces. He continues to perform as a guest artist with chamber ensembles and serves regularly on the juries of a number of international competitions. He maintains a private studio in New York City and is also an Adjunct Associate Professor of Music and Music Education at New York University. He was awarded an honorary doctorate from Shenandoah University.

www.seymourbernstein.com

NOTES